Presented to

_____

By

_____

On the Occasion of

_____

Date

_____

WHEN I'M IN HIS PRESENCE

DEVOTIONAL THOUGHTS ON WORSHIP FOR WOMEN

ANITA CORRINE DONIHUE

BARBOUR
PUBLISHING

© 2000 by Anita Corrine Donihue

ISBN 978-1-59789-865-2

All rights reserved. No part of this publication may be reproduced or transmitted in any form or by any means without written permission of the publisher.

Scripture quotations marked KJV are taken from the King James Version of the Bible.

Scripture quotations marked NKJV are taken from the New King James Version®. Copyright © 1982 by Thomas Nelson, Inc. Used by permission. All rights reserved.

Scripture quotations marked NIV are taken from the HOLY BIBLE, NEW INTERNATIONAL VERSION®, NIV®, © 1973, 1978, 1984 by International Bible Society. Used by permission of Zondervan. All rights reserved.

Published by Barbour Publishing, Inc., P.O. Box 719, Uhrichsville, Ohio 44683, www.barbourbooks.com

Our mission is to publish and distribute inspirational products offering exceptional value and biblical encouragement to the masses.

Member of the
Evangelical Christian
Publishers Association

Printed in the United States of America.

WHEN I'M IN HIS PRESENCE

Contents

INTRODUCTION

Oh, what awesome things You have done in my life, dear Lord! Everywhere I look I see miracles performed through Your presence.

Time and again You have snatched me from wrong situations. How wonderful, the way You have worked things out on my behalf.

Throughout history, You have helped when people have suffered from wars, worldwide depression, earthquakes, storms, violence, and change. Every time, Your presence has been with those who have called on Your help. Strengthening. Restoring. Healing.

Your presence surrounded great leaders in Bible times. You healed the sick and even raised people from the dead. Through the years You strengthened and comforted martyrs, gave God-fearing political leaders wisdom, brought forth great evangelists, and blessed the efforts of missionaries. You touched and restored the lives and hearts of parents and children and brought families back together again.

I praise You for how You still touch lives today as You did in the past. Thank You for being here for everyday people like me and using us in miraculous ways to fulfill Your purpose.

What good and perfect things come from Your presence. In wisdom and mercy have You done it all. Every good thing I enjoy comes from You, Lord. All that awaits me in heaven, everything that lies at my fingertips here on earth, I thank You for them. My family, friends, material possessions. Nothing compares to You and how You place Your loving hands on me. You are my all in all. You, Lord, are life itself.

Thank You for Your mighty, yet gentle, loving presence.

ASSURING

THANK YOU FOR
YOUR ASSURING PRESENCE

When I start to worry, I will refocus my thoughts on You, my Lord. Thank You for Your assuring presence, for reminding me of Your loving care. Thank You for being concerned about me.

When I start to agonize about all the things I'm forced to deal with, I look back at what You have done for me. Again, I feel You touch me with a calming assurance. Thank You, Lord, for how You show mercy and help me through when life becomes tough. Thank You for Your assuring presence during serious illnesses and even the death of a loved one. I'm learning not to be troubled about the uncertainties of these big or even little things, nor by what I will eat, drink, or wear. You already know my needs even before I ask.

I have You as my Savior. I'm alive! I will always trust in You. Instead of worrying about everything, I'm learning to tell You about everything that concerns me. Thank You ahead of time for the answers and solutions, because You know what is best for me.

When You search this land for those who trust in You, I pray You will be pleased with a heart like mine. Now I give You my worries, dear Lord. I find by trusting You, my insecurities and cares are driven away. I have peace that goes beyond all understanding, a peace of heart and mind that causes me to rest and be calm within Your assuring ways.

> *Taste and see that the LORD is good;*
> *blessed is the man who takes refuge*
> *in him.*
>
> PSALM 34:8 (NIV)

> *Cast all your anxiety on him*
> *because he cares for you.*
>
> 1 PETER 5:7 (NIV)

> *"All this I have spoken while still with you. But the Counselor, the Holy Spirit, whom the Father will send in my name, will teach you all things and will remind you of everything I have said to you. Peace I leave with you; my peace I give you. I do not give to you as the world gives. Do not let your hearts be troubled and do not be afraid."*

> *"As the Father has loved me, so have I loved you."*
>
> JOHN 14:25–27, 15:9 (NIV)

THE FALL THAT
SAVED A LIFE

New Year's Eve came and went. The following evening I left for work as usual. The company phone rang in the middle of my shift. It was for me. I heard Bruce's wife, Bobbie, speaking urgently on the other end.

"Anita, there's been an accident."

I knew my husband, Bob, had planned to visit our friend, Bruce, his wife, Bobbie, and his mother, Zelda, that night.

Bobbie went on, "Bob was getting ready to leave, when he stepped out onto our newly constructed deck that didn't have a railing yet.

"Bruce started to warn him about the ice, but it was too late. Bob slipped and fell over the side. He landed face first on some concrete blocks several feet below.

"Bruce and Zelda are taking Bob to St. Joseph's right now."

I hung up the phone and left immediately to meet them at the hospital.

When I arrived, I found Bob propped up in an emergency room hospital bed with Bruce and Zelda at his side. A cut on his forehead gaped a good inch wide and three inches long. After the doctors treated Bob, I drove him home.

The next day Bob's head had swollen to the size of a basketball, and he was in a lot of pain. I hated watching him suffer.

I rested my head on his chest and cried, asking God to help Bob. I couldn't understand why this happened. After all, doesn't God protect us?

I managed to coax Bob into seeing his family doctor. Thorough and caring, the doctor thought Bob's injury warranted a CAT scan.

The following day Bob received a call from the doctor requesting him to return to the clinic. The CAT scan showed a slow-growing brain tumor.

We had no idea. Symptoms would not normally show up from such a tumor until it would be too late. The doctor assured Bob that the accident saved his life. Had he not fallen, the CAT scan wouldn't have found the tumor in time.

Bob and I were shocked and fearful. We prayed for God to send us to the right specialists so we would know what to do next.

After an extensive search, we found a surgeon that we felt confident with at Harborview Medical Center in Seattle. It didn't take long for the three of us to opt for surgery.

Time for the surgery arrived. Our sons and their families who live locally took shifts staying with me at the hospital. Another one of our sons waited anxiously by the phone in California.

The surgery was successful. To the best of the surgical team's knowledge, the tumor was completely removed.

Our wait to see Bob in the intensive care unit seemed endless. Finally, the time came when we could be with him.

Bob forced a grin as I squeezed his hand. He was hooked up to all sorts of apparatuses. A huge bolt protruded from his head. He appeared tired and weak, but happy about the surgical team's good report.

I left for a while to have a cup of coffee and allow Bob to get some rest. Our family went home, but I remained. After a while, I returned to the intensive care waiting room. Time dragged some more until I could return to Bob's side.

I had been praying and trusting God through the whole procedure, but now my strength was dwindling.

"God, I need Your assurance and strength," I whispered.

A nurse came to the waiting room door and called my name. I could go in but not for long. Soft, indirect lights helped provide a relaxing night atmosphere in the large, quiet room. Several people in partially curtained-off areas slept restlessly. Bob faded in and out as I sat by him. I held his hand, and we prayed quietly together.

"We need Your help and assurance," I repeated to God.

A woman's sweet voice drifted softly, peacefully through the room. I couldn't see her, but her words were clear as she sang:

"I come to the garden alone. . . . And He walks with me and He talks with me. . .

" 'Tis so sweet to trust in Jesus. . .just to rest upon His promise, just to know. . .

"My Jesus, I love Thee, I know Thou art mine. . . ."

One comforting song after another wove between the patients' beds and into Bob's and my ears, assuring us of God's care and soothing our hearts.

Bob is healthy and strong, now pastoring a growing church. We still thank God for His timing in Bob's accident, for His help in the surgery, and for the comfort and assurance God gave through the sweet, beloved hymns of a woman we didn't know.

I tried to locate the woman with the lovely songs to thank her, but I wasn't successful. Instead, I thank God. I imagine God has blessed this woman already for obeying Him and being an answer to a prayer for assurance that she didn't even know she helped fulfill.

YOU ARE NEAR

When morning skies break
    and begin a new day,
    You are near.
When I give You my prayer
    and offer You praise,
    You are near.
When schedules are hectic
    and stresses are great,
    You are near.
When things don't go right,
    and I ask You for help,
    You are near.
When troubles surround me,
    and all is a loss,
    You are near.
When I do a job well with a feeling of pride,
    You are near.
When loved ones are kind, a child gives a hug,
    You are near.
When I lie down at night
    and give You my praise,
    You are near.
When sleep overtakes me until the new day,
    You are near.

ACCEPTING GOD'S ASSURANCE

Oftentimes we worry, scheme, and try to "fix" different situations in our lives or those of others instead of taking it all to the Lord and trusting Him for help and direction. God's promises are as sure now as they were when His timeless scripture was written years ago.

God assures us of His help and direction. It's a free gift He offers us. All we need to do is accept that assuring love.

We can lift our eyes to the hills and heavens beyond and seek His help. He may allow our feet to stumble, but He still guards our paths.

We have a wonderful God and Savior who never sleeps nor slumbers. Day and night He constantly watches over us, defending us against evil and harm. He protects our bodies; He also tends our souls. Not just for today, but through eternity.

Sometimes we're determined to do things our way, without first seeking God's guidance. It isn't long, however, until we're in trouble. We have to backtrack and wait as patiently as possible for His next perfect move and timing as He directs us.

God is our Rock. He's our Salvation, our Defender. When we face uncertainties and trust in Him, we will not be moved! He provides us with the steadfastness, strength, and power we need each hour, each day, month, and year.

Even when earth-shattering trials come our way, He's with us. When others let us down, He's our greatest friend. Our hope and courage lie in God, the Creator of each one of us. As we accept His assuring love, He delivers us and restores our strength and joy. All we have to do is accept and trust Him.

> *I will lift up mine eyes unto the hills,*
>   *from whence cometh my help.*
> *My help cometh from the LORD,*
>   *which made heaven and earth.*
> *He will not suffer thy foot to be moved:*
>   *he that keepeth thee will not slumber.*
> *Behold, he that keepeth Israel*
>   *shall neither slumber nor sleep.*
> *The LORD is thy keeper:*
>   *the LORD is thy shade upon thy right hand.*
> *The sun shall not smite thee by day,*
>   *nor the moon by night.*
> *The LORD shall preserve thee from all evil:*
>   *he shall preserve thy soul.*
> *The LORD shall preserve thy going out*
>   *and thy coming in from this time forth,*
>   *and even for evermore.*
>
>   PSALM 121 (KJV)

Truly my soul waiteth upon God:
from him cometh my salvation.
He only is my rock and my salvation;
he is my defence;
I shall not be greatly moved.
My soul, wait thou only upon God;
for my expectation is from him.
He only is my rock and my salvation:
he is my defence;
I shall not be moved.
In God is my salvation and my glory:
the rock of my strength,
and my refuge, is in God.
Trust in him at all times; ye people,
pour out your heart before him:
God is a refuge for us. Selah.

PSALM 62:1–2, 5–8 (KJV)

IN THE GARDEN

I come to the garden alone,
    While the dew is still on the roses;
And the voice I hear, falling on my ear,
    The Son of God discloses.

He speaks, and the sound of His voice
    Is so sweet the birds hush their singing,
And the melody that He gave to me
    Within my heart is ringing.

I'd stay in the garden with Him
    Though the night around me be falling,
But He bids me go; through the voice of woe,
    His voice to me is calling.

And He walks with me, and He talks with me,
    And He tells me I am His own;
And the joy we share as we tarry there,
    None other has ever known.

C. AUSTIN MILES, 1913

BLESSINGS

BLESSINGS ETERNAL

Thank You for the different kinds of blessings You give me, Father. Not just for material riches people often think of, but also for Your blessings that last forever.

Thank You for Your blessing of guidance. Each year I trust Your advice more. You fill my thoughts with Your heavenly purpose.

I don't have time to worry about whether I will be rich or famous in the eyes of man, because You have given me a work to do for You. I realize life is short, Lord. I can't waste it. Help me budget my time like a carefully balanced bankbook. When I accomplish a little more for Your kingdom, I feel wealthier than a millionaire.

Thank You for blessing me with a heart filled with joy. How rich I feel to hear Your call to serve. Because of this, I place my spiritual treasures in heaven. Nothing can snatch them away, nor do they rust or wear out. Your spiritual treasures will even last beyond this fragile physical life of mine and go on forever!

I don't know if You will grant me worldly riches. If You do, I will praise You and try to be a good steward. My focus is on You, my Lord, not on love of money. I enjoy the material blessings You grant me, but I don't want to become corrupt and make them my idol.

Your blessings are more wonderful than the finest gems! Thank You for them. Please help me remember throughout my life to invest in heavenly things and keep my heart fixed there.

Through all this, I praise You for material blessings, comfort and ease and joy indescribable. How amazing it is when I pass some of these blessings on to others. You return them to me, pressed down and overflowing with Your love.

I love those who love me,
and those who seek me find me.
With me are riches and honor,
enduring wealth and prosperity.
My fruit is better than fine gold;
what I yield surpasses choice silver.
I walk in the way of righteousness,
along the paths of justice,
bestowing wealth on those who love me
and making their treasuries full.

PROVERBS 8:17–21 (NIV)

Look for the Little Things

Are you searching for God's blessings,
    Trying hard to find just one?
Are you walking in the shadows,
    Hanging on 'til day is done?

Do you fail to see the wonder,
    That God offers you each day?
Do you notice all He bestows?
    All the joy He sends your way?

God gives many kinds of blessings,
    Through the little things we see.
He turns shadows into sunlight,
    Hued with rainbow, rose, and tree.

God breaks dullness with bright laughter,
    Or a child's sweet, simple deed.
He grants wonders unexpectedly.
    His surprises meet each need.

When you notice the little things—
   His blessings, all around,
When you're glad for what each day brings,
   Then your happiness abounds.

Feel caresses from spring breezes,
   Smell the freshness in His rain.
Step out at night and watch the stars,
   Shoot across the sky again.

Arise before the sun comes up,
   View a glorious orange display,
Revealing waking signs of life,
   That welcome a brand-new day.

Keep looking for the little things.
   God's blessings will come to you,
Filling your heart with peace and joy,
   And making your life brand-new.

Thank You for the Little Blessings

Father, sometimes I go along full speed ahead, not looking right or left. I may forget to look up to You and be aware of Your small blessings. Numerous things I must accomplish (or seemingly so) crowd out the most important gifts You have planned.

Please remind me, Lord, to keep watching for Your everyday miniblessings. When I'm buried under responsibilities and feel life just isn't all that great, I want to be mindful of the little things keeping the joy in my life.

Perhaps simple, split-second blessings in a busy day are more than insignificant. They often turn out to be the most treasured times of my life.

Thank You, Lord.

BUTTERFLY BLESSINGS

Years ago when our sons Bob Jr. and Dan were five and six, we often came upon the simple miracles of nature. No matter how busy, we managed to stop and take in the special events.

One day we discovered a tiny green caterpillar in the yard. The boys gathered a wide-mouthed quart jar from our porch pantry. I broke a small branch from a tree. We held it close enough so the caterpillar could creep onto it. We gently placed the branch in the jar and poked holes in a lid for the top.

I was fortunate to be a stay-at-home mommy during this time, so it made our project easier to add drops of water to the branch each day and keep a close watch on the little green creature.

We were all delighted when the caterpillar began busily spinning its cocoon. Bobby, Danny, and I marveled at the way it knew exactly what to do. It looked like God's finger helped balance the bottom tip of the cocoon as it spun round and round.

We kept a closer watch after that, so the developing

butterfly would be able to live and fly away when it broke out of its silky case.

The boys peered anxiously through the glass at what looked like a lifeless green form. They wondered if anything would happen.

Finally the day arrived. The now swollen cocoon began to wiggle. I called the boys immediately.

We took the jar out to our yard and carefully removed the lid. Slowly, gently, I lifted the branch from the jar and balanced it on the rim with my index finger and thumb. The sack hung off to one side, where it continued to wriggle and began slowly splitting. The boys gasped and whispered with delight, afraid of disturbing the wondrous process.

Before long, a beautiful monarch butterfly emerged, appearing wet and exhausted. The fresh, new creature opened its glorious newly formed wings ever so slowly. It lifted them up, then down in a laboring, rhythmic motion. With each movement, the butterfly appeared stronger. Again, I could almost see that God had splashed vivid colors on the lovely creature and helped lift and lower its wings as they dried.

New power filled the caterpillar-turned-butterfly. With one big thrust, it took to the air. We watched it go as though we were bidding a small friend farewell.

Witnessing the blessing of this butterfly has been

only part of the miracle. Now Bob Jr. and Dan are grown men, married, and have blessed my husband and me with daughters-in-law and grandchildren. There are many times Bob and I stand back in awe as we witness the gentle, God-loving way these big, strong men and their wives teach their children the miracles of nature and how to respect them.

I'll never forget the blessing of that butterfly and the lessons God taught me: to stop and enjoy the little things of life.

I will exalt you, my God the King;
    I will praise your name for ever and ever.
Every day I will praise you
    and extol your name for ever and ever.

Great is the LORD and most worthy of praise;
    his greatness no one can fathom.
One generation will commend
    your works to another;
        they will tell of your mighty acts.
They will speak of the glorious splendor
    of your majesty,
    and I will meditate on your
    wonderful works.
They will tell of the power of
    your awesome works,
    and I will proclaim your great deeds.
They will celebrate your abundant goodness
    and joyfully sing of your righteousness.

The LORD is gracious and compassionate,
    slow to anger and rich in love.
The LORD is good to all;
    he has compassion on all he has made.

PSALM 145:1–9 (NIV)

ROYAL BLUE PERFORMANCE

The day was like any other. The time, early afternoon. Bob and I had driven to a routine doctor's appointment for me about ten miles from our home. As usual, we were exceptionally busy and wanted a little extra time together. Taking the old river road home seemed a nice way to gear down.

Sun rays splintered through the clouds and reflected off a soft haze hovering over the river. Bob and I drank in the tranquillity.

As we rounded a bend, a four-foot blue heron stood eloquently by the roadside. We slowed to a near stop. The royal-colored bird spread its huge wings and gracefully glided above the river. It maneuvered itself to fly parallel with our car windows. Soon the huge bird must have spotted a fish. Its trim body angled perfectly, and it dove out of sight.

We were exhilarated and felt the stress-induced tension slip from our bodies. The entertainment from a magnificent blue heron surpassed anything we had witnessed for a long time.

Bob and I still talk about the river drive and the lovely blue heron. For years we had simply tried to get a glimpse of one through our binoculars in a local protected nesting area. Instead, God chose to bless us that day with a front-row (car) seat, full-view, personal performance.

NOTICING GOD'S BLESSINGS

Do you ever find yourself trudging from one day to the next unaware of the simple blessings God sends your way? Like Eeyore, Winnie the Pooh's gloomy friend, do you ever force a smile, then greet others with a mournful salutation?

The age-old song "Count Your Blessings" is a wonderful therapy. It will shake off the hohums and stress. The words mentally flow like a revolving turntable.

Think of when you have been blessed by a full rainbow after a storm. The lightning boomed. Trees, plants, animals, and people succumbed to the pelting rain; then a colorful rainbow broke through.

Recall when you awoke to the most remarkable

sunrise ever and heard birds chirping outside your window. You smelled the morning dew. Later you viewed a gorgeous sunset.

What a delight to watch a child make a simple discovery and witness a look of amazement on that little one's face. How refreshing it is to see an elderly man and woman walking hand in hand.

The phone rings or a letter arrives and makes your day. You hear a favorite song or an amusing story on the car radio. It may give you a lift that can last for hours.

These are God's everyday blessings. Savor them. Pull them up from your memory log and be doubly blessed.

When someone speaks sharply or cuts you off on the freeway, when worries pile up, think on these wonderful things.

Bob and I love the ocean. Every time we go, he finds a stick, draws a big heart in the sand, and puts our initials in it.

When things seem stressful, I hear God remind me of the blue heron or Bob's heart in the sand.

My Song Shall Be of Jesus

My song shall be of Jesus,
    His mercy crowns my days;
He fills my cup with blessings
    And tunes my heart to praise.

My song shall be of Jesus,
    The precious Lamb of God,
Who gave Himself my ransom
    And bought me with His blood.

My song shall be of Jesus,
    When, sitting at His feet,
I call to mind His goodness,
    In meditation sweet.

My song shall be of Jesus,
  Whatever ill betide;
I'll sing the grace that saves me
  And keeps me at His side.

My song shall be of Jesus,
  While pressing on my way
To reach the blissful region
  Of pure and perfect day.

And when my soul shall enter
  The gate of Eden fair,
A song of praise to Jesus
  I'll sing forever there.

FRANCES JANE (FANNY) CROSBY, late 1800s

COUNT YOUR BLESSINGS

When upon life's billows you are tempest tossed,
When you are discouraged, thinking all is lost,
Count your many blessings—
    name them one by one,
And it will surprise you
    what the Lord hath done.

Are you ever burdened with a load of care?
Does the cross seem heavy
    you are called to bear?
Count your many blessings—
    every doubt will fly,
And you will keep singing
    as the days go by.

When you look at others
    with their lands and gold,
Think that Christ has promised you
    His wealth untold;
Count your many blessings—
    money cannot buy
Your reward in heaven nor your home on high.

So, amid the conflict, whether great or small,
Do not be discouraged—God is over all;
Count your many blessings—
    angels will attend,
Help and comfort give you
    to your journey's end.

Count your blessings—name them one by one;
Count your blessings see what God has done.

JOHNSON OATMAN JR., 1897

CALLING

HEARING GOD'S CALLS

How can we hear God calling us in this crazy, tumultuous world? Each day is like a roller coaster. We never slow down.

God has an uncanny ability of speaking to us in quiet and hectic moments. Our problem is that we forget to keep our focus on Him. It is only in doing so that we recognize God's calls when they come. We must walk and talk with Him throughout our day. When the Bible tells us to pray without ceasing, it doesn't mean we have to spend the entire time kneeling in our quiet place. But how wonderful it is when we can; these opportunities don't come often. I believe the Bible encourages us to talk and listen to God wherever we go, whatever we do. It's the same as we do with a best friend. The more we listen to Him and read His word, the more likely we will recognize His voice when He does call. God may call us from life's restless seas, from our comfortable spot in a plush church pew, or from our favorite living room chair. He may call us to our heart's desire or to leave our comfort zone. No matter what His call, God knows us well and takes our concerns to heart.

God may call us to different things. Perhaps He wants us to become ministers, missionaries, doctors, or teachers, but God needs Christian people in many walks of life. Through His calling and guidance, we can make a difference.

In every line of work, every area of our day, God leads us to important things needing to be done. By listening to His direction, the deeds we do will often bring wonderful blessings. They are the callings God gives us to do little and big things. He frequently asks us to serve with no benefits except the rewards of a warm heart. God might urge us to teach a church school class, sing in the choir, bring flowers for the sanctuary, or clean and repair the church. The list of many needs goes on. Sometimes we feel His Holy Spirit touch our hearts to write letters, visit the sick, make phone calls, or simply let that frantic driver squeeze in front of us in a traffic jam! God may direct us to listen to a young person who tells us things we don't want to hear. He may then encourage us to listen some more and love them right where they are. He might urge us to bake goodies for someone, provide free babysitting, mow the neighbor's lawn, or shovel snow.

God calls us to serve as He served. Let's pray for Him to help us never be too "good" for our Master's simple tasks. Instead, let us give Him our best whether or not it is convenient.

When we follow His call, we sow seeds of kindness

and reap a harvest of rejoicing. May God then look at us and say, "Well done, my child."

And He said to them, "Follow Me, and I will make you fishers of men." They immediately left their nets and followed Him.

MATTHEW 4:19–20 (NKJV)

Preach the Word; be prepared in season and out of season; correct, rebuke and encourage—with great patience and careful instruction. For the time will come when men will not put up with sound doctrine. Instead, to suit their own desires, they will gather around them a great number of teachers to say what their itching ears want to hear. They will turn their ears away from the truth and turn aside to myths. But you, keep your head in all situations, endure hardship, do the work of an evangelist, discharge all the duties of your ministry.

[Be ready to say someday,] I have fought the good fight, I have finished the race, I have kept the faith. Now there is in store for me the crown of righteousness, which the Lord, the righteous Judge, will award to me on that day—and not

only to me, but also to all who have longed for his appearing.

2 TIMOTHY 4:2–5, 7–8 (NIV)

I HEED YOUR CALL

I love You, Lord Jesus. I long to do what You ask of me. Now, as I kneel in prayer, I know You are calling me to this work for You.

Thank You for choosing an everyday, average person like me. Am I worthy? Do I have the knowledge or abilities to accomplish this task You are calling me to? You must see beyond my limited understanding. You are all-wise and all-knowing.

I won't dwell on the "what-ifs" and "how-tos," but simply lay each one before You and trust You to work out the details.

Thank You for preparing me for this moment. I praise You for calling me to serve You. I give You my all. I won't look back but will go forward in obedience and unswerving faith in You, my Almighty God.

Here I am, Lord, send me.

Then said Jesus to them again, Peace be unto you:
as my Father hath sent me, even so send I you.

JOHN 20:21 (KJV)

PURE HEART
IN THE SLUMS

Born in 1910, she was given the name Agnes Gonxha Bojaxhiu. She lived with her loving family in Skopje, Yugoslavia. She was a happy child and loved school and church.

By the time she turned twelve, she felt God calling her to become a missionary. When she reached eighteen, she knew God wanted her to help in India.

She began teaching high school students in Calcutta. Before long, she became a principal of the school.

One night God gave Agnes a vision. She saw poor and sick people all around her. God was calling her to serve in the slums of Calcutta. She helped and helped until she had given away all her earthly possessions.

God provided a way for her to open a home and rescue homeless children from the dirty, rat-filled streets. The number of children soon turned to over forty. Individuals she had served in the past came to help at the home.

Because of the severe needs, the city donated a building that would be made into a hospital for poor people. She named the hospital Nirmal Hriday, which means "pure heart."

People around the world joined her crusade to help the needy. She started orphanages, schools, hospitals, and helped provide missions with food and a village for those who had leprosy.

Her mission spread throughout the entire world, including the United States. Some referred to her as the "saint of the gutters." She believed what we do isn't as important as the love we put into it.

In 1979, she was given the Nobel Peace Prize. She used the award money to help the poor.

Throughout her life, Mother Teresa aided thousands of poverty-stricken people. Some felt the problem was so great, her work was only a drop in the ocean. Mother Teresa felt the ocean was made up of many drops.

Many thank God for the unselfish love and service given by Mother Teresa and others who help the poor.

Jesus Calls Us

Jesus calls us over the tumult
  Of life's wild, restless, sea;
Day by day His sweet voice soundeth,
  Saying, "Christian, follow Me!"

Jesus calls us from the worship
  Of the vain world's golden store,
From each idol that would keep us,
  Saying, "Christian, love Me more!"

In our joys and in our sorrows,
  Days of toil and hours of ease,
Still He calls, in cares and pleasures,
  "Christian, love Me more than these!"

Jesus calls us! By thy mercies,
  Saviour may we hear Thy call,
Give our hearts to Thine obedience,
  Serve and love Thee best of all.

CECIL FRANCES ALEXANDER, 1852

SHOWING ME HOW TO SERVE

The ways You lead me are not always ones I would desire, Lord. Hearkening to Your call may be a struggle. The tasks You give are at times unpleasant, difficult, and exhausting. Still, I thank You for Your calling me to serve You and for giving me the strength to follow.

I want to be a willing servant, one like You were here on earth. When I'm tempted to complain about the homage I must give, I thank You for reminding me how You sacrificed even more. When my energy droops and I want to give up, I'm reminded of how faithful You are. My burdens are never so heavy that I sweat great drops of blood. You haven't asked me to give my life for all humankind.

Because I love You so much, I won't seek ease and prestige, but will rather be an obedient servant for You.

Thank You, Lord, for showing me how to serve. In light of Your holiness and unlimited love, I feel humbled. When the job seems thankless, I recall how You wrapped a towel around Your waist. You knelt as a servant and washed the dirty, sweaty feet of Your disciples. Not only those who loved You, but the ones who would deny and betray You. Did You see beyond the disease, the dirt and grime, the sin and tragedy to a miraculous, triumphant plan lying ahead? Did Your love really make it possible to forgive our faults in spite of knowing full well You were about to give Your life for us? I can't comprehend it all.

Thank You, Lord, for showing me how to serve in any capacity and for giving me a vision of what You want accomplished. It doesn't matter how hard the task or who gets the credit. What matters is that I be used by You, my Master and my Savior. I will serve You anytime, anywhere. I'm grateful for Your always being near and showing me how to serve in each job You give me. Through this process, I feel a growing warmth in my heart. Your blessings overflow within me.

"Do you understand what I have done for you?" he asked them. "You call me 'Teacher' and 'Lord,' and rightly so, for that is what I am. Now that I, your Lord and Teacher, have washed your feet, you also should wash one another's feet. I have set you an example that you should do as I have done for you. I tell you the truth, no servant is greater than his master, nor is a messenger greater than the one who sent him. Now that you know these things, you will be blessed if you do them."

JOHN 13:12–17 (NIV)

REAPING DAY BY DAY

Working in the smiling field of life from day to
day,
Trying hard to save all the golden grain;
With our songs of Jesus keeping shadows all
away,
True to our Redeemer we remain.

Keeping us from evil He is with us all day long,
Giving what we need, blessing what we do;
Lovingly He tells us we shall sing the triumph
song,
If we labor on with courage true.

Praise His name forever! To His promise we
will cling
Till our labors end at the gates of light;
Then He will reward us for the sheaves that we
shall bring,
With a word of praise and welcome bright.

WILL R. KELLY, 1916

THE IMPOSSIBLE CALLING

Bob worked long, hard hours through our early years of marriage. This made it possible for me to work part-time so I could be home more with our children. Now our five sons are grown men; two are married with families.

With the children grown, I felt compelled to take on a second job for only a couple of years. I had been a teacher's assistant in our local school district for years, so we opted for an opposite type with convenient hours: fast-food work. That wouldn't be too difficult, we thought.

Fast-food work was difficult and challenging. It often left me exhausted, but I was determined to stick it out.

Before long, we discovered why God had sent me to this task. We discovered Bob's brain tumor. Although the doctors had successfully removed the tumor, Bob's strength became limited for quite a while.

Between both jobs, I worked about sixty-five hours per week. Many thought I would never be able to continue but God gave me the strength I needed for each day. I thanked Him for providing the work to help us through. I often hummed the tune "The Joy of the Lord Is My Strength" to and from both jobs.

We praised God when Bob regained his health. He was able to return to the ministry and accepted the pastorate of a small church. It began rapidly growing. I offered to continue my work schedule for a while longer.

I felt God near. He watered and fed my soul each day. He whispered words of encouragement and planted a seed. Before long, the seed grew into a calling. God wanted me to write for His glory. Not just for my enjoyment, but for others to read. I wondered if He had called me to write one magazine article. I felt that would be wonderful.

I began my search for a teacher who could guide me. Not just any teacher—a Christian teacher, or at least someone who would be receptive about my writing for the Lord. I found nothing. I refused to give up. Instead, I kept working, praying, and scanning the college flyers.

One evening, a woman walked into the fast-food restaurant and ordered her meal. While she ate, I cleaned the dining room. We struck up a conversation. It turned out that she worked in the office of a local college. I expressed my desire about writing and how I couldn't find the instructor I needed. In one moment, the woman gave me information that changed my life. She knew someone, an instructor and author named Colleen L. Reece.

I found Colleen's phone number and called her

the next morning from my second-grade classroom. It didn't take long during our conversation for me to realize Colleen was a Christian. I was thrilled, to say the least!

The next college quarter arrived. I had two nights off at the fast-food restaurant. I arranged for one night to be used for the writing class. Colleen took the seedling of my calling and nurtured it. She challenged me to learn and grow. She encouraged me to do all I could plus a little more.

One evening after class a group of us walked to our cars. I told Colleen I had a strong feeling God wanted me to write a book about prayer. I thought it might sound far-fetched to her. Instead, Colleen took me seriously and told me something I will never forget.

"Treat it like a third job, Anita. Keep going and don't give up."

When I told my friends I wanted to write, some believed me. Others rolled their eyes. A few even advised me to be realistic or implied it would never happen. The discouraging comments and snickers didn't deter me, because I knew God was calling and that He would help me.

The most wonderful part was the love and encouragement I received from my husband and family. They told me to hang on to my vision and said they knew I could do it.

I felt God reminding me to be careful and wise in what I chose to write. The responsibility He was placing on my shoulders was overwhelming. One night during evening church service, I asked for prayer that God would grant me the wisdom I needed. I was anointed with oil. The saints gathered around and prayed. None of us imagined the spiritual blessings God had in store.

Four years passed. Each year I arranged for one night off from my night job so I could take Colleen's class. I became involved with a writers' group filled with positive, encouraging people.

Magazine articles I wrote were being accepted. I was able to cut my night job back to three nights a week, instead of five.

Fatigue continued to take its toll. Still God gave me strength to write. The words burned in my mind. I couldn't get them down on paper fast enough. Colleen remained closer than ever, continually coaxing me not to give up.

I was delighted when Colleen and I coauthored two gift books for teachers and one on holidays. We were blessed along with our readers as *Apples for a Teacher*, *Joy to the World*, and *A Teacher's Heart* went out to the stores.

Finally, my book on prayer was well under way. I sent out a book proposal three times with no success. I kept praying for guidance and felt the Lord continuing to lead. I submitted it to Barbour Publishing. I was delighted when the answer came back, "yes."

When I'm on My Knees, we would call it. I saw the beginning of a new fork in my spiritual road. How humbling. How overwhelming. After that, God helped me write another, *When I'm Praising God.*

I'm nearing the end of working two jobs now. God has shown me a way to leave the fast-food work behind so I can put more time into writing for Him.

I'm sharing this story with you for a reason. Perhaps it will remind you never to give up on God's leading. He has His own timing and way of accomplishing His call for us. He even gives us the strength and direction we need. Oftentimes we are forced to persevere or be patient and not get ahead of His will.

When we trust in Him, God puts the right Christian people in our paths. I thank God for how He continues to touch and bless me through His faithful servant and my friend Colleen, and my dear family.

He sends me other Christians, too. I am blessed by kind actions, words, letters, and phone calls as I continue along God's path.

When God touches your heart to serve Him, trust and obey. Then watch the exciting adventure unfold.

FROM MUSH TO MIGHT

My brain turns to mush and my knees become jelly, Lord, when it comes time to tell people about the wonderful things You do for me. Talking with those who know You as their Savior is easy. The ones who don't know You sometimes make me shake in my boots.

This is when I gulp and call on You for help. Thank You, Lord, for turning my mush into might. A tremendous power that comes from You gives me the right words to speak at the right time. I praise You for Your strengthening presence, because I'm not so strong on my own.

I'm grateful when You help me tell anyone and everyone who will listen. Even though I'm afraid they may brush me off or laugh, I still want to share how You saved me and recount the good news of all the awesome things You do.

I count it a privilege to be one of Your

ambassadors. Let me win many souls for You, Lord, so they also can know You and have a life of joy and peace, free from sin.

I recall Your command for all who believe in You: to tell everyone we can about the gospel, the good news of Your saving grace.

Thank You for Your gentle touch as You teach me step-by-step how I can lead someone to You. I praise You when someone makes a decision to become a Christian. You step in and guide them with Your transforming love and power.

I don't save people. You do. How awesome! How wonderful.

When the next time comes to tell someone my story about You, I already thank You for giving me a quick mind, a loving heart, firm knees, and intestinal fortitude so I can take a deep breath and tell of Your love.

BRINGING IN THE SHEAVES

Sowing in the morning, sowing seeds of
    kindness,
Sowing in the noontide and the dewy eve;
Waiting for the harvest, and the time of
    reaping,
We shall come rejoicing, bringing in the
    sheaves.

Sowing in the sunshine, sowing in the shadows,
Fearing neither clouds nor winter's
    chilling breeze;
By and by the harvest, and the labor ended,
We shall come rejoicing, bringing in the
    sheaves.

Going forth with weeping, sowing for the
    Master,
Though the loss sustained our spirit often
    grieves;
When our weeping's over, He will bid us
    welcome,
We shall come rejoicing, bringing in the
    sheaves.

KNOWLES SHAW, 1874

CALMING

YOUR CALMNESS

In this world filled with stress, trials, and uncertainties, a calm spirit is often unknown, Lord. In spite of this, I realize peace does not come from circumstances. Instead, it's a condition of the heart.

Though pressure flurries surround me, I thank You for Your abiding presence, the source of calm, deep within my soul. When conflicts arise, I must remember to pray. Your steady, calm voice unwinds my emotions.

I have learned that only the humble and patient inherit the earth and enjoy this wonderful freedom from stress. I won't let unkind words or anyone's thoughtless actions get under my skin. With Your help, I'll quietly keep my thoughts fixed on You, the source of peace. When snap decisions must be made, I feel You slow my racing thoughts so I can reason things out logically and handle them in a harmonious manner.

When pressures come, I cry for Your help, and You answer. You grant strength and bless me with peace of heart and mind. Help me each time, Lord, to turn from the easy reaction of handling things impatiently to pursuing Your right way. Through it all, I feel You give me a calm, cool head once again.

When I need an escape, thank You for providing refuge where I can get away for a short while. (Even if it's only a walk around the block!) Thank You for how You protect my emotions and my inner being. You fill me with songs of joy and peace.

This calmness that comes only from Your touch, Lord, goes beyond any understanding. It keeps my heart and soul close to You, for You are the foundation and the source of any real peace.

Thank You, Lord, for how You give me peace during the busiest moments of my life. Not a peace as the world gives, but one that comes from Your Holy Spirit.

Please, keep helping me not to be troubled or afraid. I believe in You, for You are my God, my source of calmness.

"Peace I leave with you; my peace I give you. I do not give to you as the world gives. Do not let your hearts be troubled and do not be afraid."
JOHN 14:27 (NIV)

A CALMING WAY

My Uncle Russell and Aunt Dorothy have a calming way about them. It isn't anything you can really put your finger on. It's just there. It comes in the way of a smile, a joke, or their simply being there for someone to love and feel loved in return. Almost everyone who knows them feels it.

Perhaps it's the history they've seen. Their ways remind me that the problems we face in this crazy world aren't new. People have survived through the ages.

Russell leans back in his easy chair, his hands clasped behind his head. He purses his lips. His eyes twinkle. He listens and listens some more. Best of all, he understands.

Dorothy laughs a lot. The trill in her joyful laughter sounds like a tinkling bell or wind chimes on a breezy day.

Her cheerful manner reminds me, *Things will work out. You'll see.* She's great at constantly pointing out the brighter side. She sets a cup of tea at your fingertips and tells wonderful stories to lift your spirits.

Funny thing. After a while, it all does fall into place! The calm chases anxiety and uncertainties out their welcome door.

I'm thankful for Uncle Russell and Aunt Dorothy and their calming, reassuring ways. Their love wraps around me like a warm blanket and makes me feel relaxed and secure.

GOD'S CALMING WAY

When the trials, temptations, uncertainties, and anxieties of this fast-paced society beat around us like a one-hundred-mile-an-hour hurricane, we can cling to the solid Rock, Jesus Christ.

There is something about the way He pulls us into the eye of the storm, where we are forced to sit still, listen, and feel His calming presence.

I can't understand how He does it. He just has a way of surrounding us with peace when we stop what we're frantically doing and cry, "Here, Lord, is all my stress, my crazy schedule, my temptations, and worries. Please help me."

We hand it all over like a desperate office manager does with his or her secretary, and we anxiously wait for everything to be sorted out and put in the right order. Afterward we sigh with relief and are grateful.

Life's hardships are far more important than a stack

of papers. The Savior, of course, is far greater than one efficient secretary. He is order and wisdom. He is all-knowing.

Best of all is the peace and calm that follow after we release everything and let God take control with His calming, guiding touch.

> *In the shelter of your presence*
> *you hide them.*
>
> PSALM 31:20 (NIV)

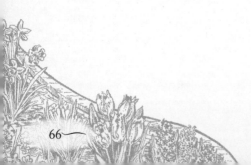

BEAUTIFUL MUSIC

Thank You, Lord, for the beautiful music in
    my life.
The whistling teakettle in the early
    morning chill.
The soft, whooshing of the furnace
    blowing warm air through the house.
The chirp of an energetic robin outside our
    window.
The purring of our kitty awaiting his breakfast.
The singing of my husband in the
    shower.
The Christian music on the radio when I'm on
    my way to work.
The still, ever presence of Your voice
    throughout the day.
The tender greeting from my husband after
    work.
The kids wrestling and playing in the evening.
The soft tone of my sons before bed, "Good
    night, Mom. I love you."
I hear my echo. "I love you, too."

JESUS, LOVER OF MY SOUL

Jesus, Lover of my soul,
  Let me to Thy bosom fly,
While the nearer waters roll,
  While the tempest still is high:
Hide me, O my Saviour, hide
  Till the storm of life is past,
Safe into the haven guide,
  O receive my soul at last!

Other refuge have I none;
  Hangs my helpless soul on Thee;
Leave, ah! leave me not alone,
  Still support and comfort me!
All my trust on Thee is stay'd,
  All my help from Thee I bring:
Cover my defenceless head
  With the shadow of Thy wing!

Plenteous grace with Thee is found,
    Grace to cover all my sin;
Let the healing streams abound;
    Make and keep me pure within:
Thou of Life the Fountain art,
    Freely let me take of Thee;
Spring Thou up within my heart,
    Rise to all eternity!

CHARLES WESLEY, 1740

THE SHELTER OF
YOUR PRESENCE

In the shelter of Your presence
    You allow my soul to hide.
There You teach me many lessons
    As You keep me by Your side.

Stress and turmoil won't destroy me
    Though the storms and tempests come.
I've a shelter in Your presence
    Where You welcome me back home.

CHRISTIAN

THE BODY OF CHRIST

Thank You, Father, for every Christian. Each one makes up Your holy church, the body of Christ: forgiven, representing Your wonderful love.

Thank You for Your Son, Jesus, who is the cornerstone of the church. He binds us together as Christians and makes the true church of the living God.

As believers, we are not limited to time or space. Neither have You separated us into doctrines or creeds. This was our doing. Only through You, Father, are we one in Christ.

Wherever I go, my heart skips a beat when I come across fellow Christians. There is a spirit about them. Your Spirit. It communes between us and causes us to recognize each other as brothers and sisters in the Lord.

Thank You for the power of Your Holy Spirit who binds us together in Your love.

CHRIST, THE CORNERSTONE

The church is built on Christ, the Rock.
    He alone is the cornerstone.
When the church weathers mighty storms
    And turns her attention to Christ,
He overcomes sin and restores peace.

Blest Be the Tie That Binds

Blest be the tie that binds
    Our hearts in Christian love;
The fellowship of kindred minds
    Is like to that above.

Before our Father's throne
    We pour our ardent prayers;
Our fears, our hopes, our aims are one,
    Our comforts and our cares.

We share each other's woes,
    Each other's burdens bear;
And often for each other flows
    The sympathizing tear.

From sorrow, toil, and pain,
    And sin we shall be free;
And perfect love and joy shall reign
    Through all eternity.

JOHN FAWCETT, 1782

Let love be without dissimulation. Abhor that which is evil; cleave to that which is good. Be kindly affectioned one to another with brotherly love; in honour preferring one another. Not slothful in business; fervent in spirit; serving the Lord; rejoicing in hope; patient in tribulation; continuing instant in prayer; distributing to the necessity of saints; given to hospitality. Bless them which persecute you: bless, and curse not. Rejoice with them that do rejoice, and weep with them that weep. Be of the same mind one toward another.

ROMANS 12:9–16 (KJV)

THE CHRISTIAN FAMILY

Many of us love and appreciate our genealogical families. The bloodline ties are strong. The memories built are loved and cherished.

There is another kind of family. It's broader than the Jones or Smith family. It is the Christian family, one made by God, our Father. Here, too, is a strong bond of love.

We often refer to one another as brothers and sisters in Christ. Some members of the Christian family help parent the younger. Others form friendships that last a lifetime.

What causes this spiritual family bond with ties lasting into eternity? The bond comes from God adopting each of us as His own children. He pours out a love that spreads from one of us to the other. He often blesses people with His presence by working through the believers in His Christian family.

Love in God's family can even go as deep as our genealogical one. Frequently, praise God, the two interweave.

The family is God's holy church. It may be shaken, split by division, or injured by illness or death. With God's healing presence, His family is restored and goes on.

The greatest miracle is that we are not forever separated. We can look forward to being reunited with Christ in heaven.

A New Heritage

Nine-year-old Jerry didn't have a happy home life. His father left when Jerry was four. His mother spent most of her time drinking and doing drugs. He felt little or no love come his way. Jerry was struggling to take care of himself.

A neighbor across the street took an interest in the young boy and started taking him to church every week. The church began loving Jerry as one of their own. Families often invited him to Sunday dinner and took him on fun family outings with their children. Others gave him gifts, such as a jacket "that just happened to be on sale."

The church's love bore fruit. When Jerry became a teenager, he grew to realize there was something more in life than the poor examples set by his parents. A new longing came into his heart: to know the God he had learned about through the years. Jerry shed tears of joy when he prayed with his pastor and invited Jesus into his heart. Soon Jerry became active in his church, but something was still missing. He felt a terrible void. His parents didn't know or seem to care about the Lord.

Jerry returned to his pastor for advice. They talked and prayed about his concern. "I feel my church is more of a family than any of my relatives," Jerry said sorrowfully.

His pastor smiled and chose his words carefully. "You have a family, Jerry, that needs your continuing, compassionate love. You also have a Christian family that gives you a heritage that can fill that void. It will help you love and understand your parents more than ever. You belong to Christ Jesus. When you became a Christian, you were adopted into God's family."

Then the pastor turned to Psalm 27:10 NIV in the Bible and read, "Though my father and mother forsake me, the Lord will receive me." A flame of hope and understanding ignited in Jerry.

From then on, Jerry saw things in a new light. He felt thankful that God had passed His love on to him through the love and prayers of Christian friends.

Although he never quit loving and praying for his parents, Jerry knew he had a heritage in his Christian family, too, the family of God.

POWER OF LOVE

D. L. Moody tells of a little boy from Chicago who went to a mission Sunday school near his home. The boy's family had to move five miles away.

Still, every Sunday the small boy walked five miles to the church he loved. A woman from a nearby church noticed the boy walking each Sunday and asked him why he didn't attend a Sunday school close to home. She explained that many other churches were just as good.

"I do because they love a fellow over there," the boy explained.

Many of us want more than a place to worship. We thrive on God's loving touch, which comes from the Christians in God's church.

BURDEN BEARERS

Did you know people in Christian leadership have burdens just like everyone else? Many appear to be strong, always ready to lift others up. Unfortunately, few share their cares and needs. They are always trying to be encouragers to those around them.

Instead of telling their needs, Christian leaders frequently pour out their hearts to God in their private prayer closets. They await His answers while continuing to work in God's service.

This is where we as Christians come in. A short note

to your pastor and his wife, an encouraging word for your song leader or church school teachers, and prayers for all of them add a multitude of blessings.

Burdens of these workers for the Lord are often many. Each good deed turns into a touch from God and pumps a renewed spirit into them.

Recently, I felt buried in a workload up to my ears. The tasks were tremendous. I longed for more time to write. My spirits drooped along with my physical strength. I took my problem to the Lord and asked Him for encouragement.

A few days later it arrived by mail in the form of an uplifting note from a friend, assuring me of her prayers. It was awesome how she felt God had placed not only me but my husband, as well, on her heart to pray for and wrote us a note.

Bob and I are always thankful for these times of encouragement. Needless to say, my friend's note kicked some energy and enthusiasm into me.

Along with receiving the blessings freely given, please remember to cheer and strengthen your spiritual leaders. You can make a difference for them, and they will be thankful.

OUR CHRISTIAN YOUTH

I love watching our outstanding Christian young people. They are hope for our future. I marvel at how smart, well-informed, perceptive, and more physically fit these kids are than what I recall from my younger years.

The world often notices bad reports about teenagers. I'm thankful for God touching our lives with the ones who plod along in Christian love day after day, attempting to make a difference in life. I'm also thankful for adults who are quick in praising kids who do well, even with the little accomplishments.

What a blessing when we use Christian youth in our churches. As we train them to become future teachers, choir directors, board members, and even pastors, God honors our efforts. He helps us be Christian examples for them in attitude, reliability, and consistency. He reminds us to flee from negative responses and squabbles. Instead, we can be grateful for how God gives us insight to understand the growing pains these kids have. He teaches us to pass unconditional love on to them. We may forget the way we felt in our teenage years, how we also faced difficulties.

I can't imagine how much harder it is to grow

up in these times. My heart breaks at what young people have to deal with. Let's pray for God to grant them strength. May He help them become victorious winners in their walks with Him, and may they give Him all the glory. May we be quick to show love and lend a helping hand, to listen more and try to understand how they feel.

How exciting it is to see the zest and enthusiasm in our youth, when one by one they give their hearts to God. Look at the joy given through their testimonies! Thank God for each one as He uses them to touch lives and win souls.

Elderly Prayer Warriors

How priceless are the elderly Christian prayer warriors and the wisdom they share. We can be grateful for their steadfast prayers, carrying out miracle after miracle. When we're willing to listen, God uses these Christian veterans and helps us build on their experiences, good and bad.

Some are never ready to retire from working in God's kingdom. How beautiful are they who adopt the younger ones, as they give loving, nourishing care.

May we someday become fruitful, laboring elders who are a blessing in years to come.

My son, keep your father's commands
and do not forsake your mother's teaching.
Bind them upon your heart forever;
fasten them around your neck.

When you walk, they will guide you;
when you sleep, they will watch over you;
when you awake, they will speak to you.

For these commands are a lamp,
this teaching is a light,
and the corrections of discipline
are the way to life.

PROVERBS 6:20–23 (NIV)

HAVE YOU A SONG?

Have you a song, a little song
    To cheer a brother's way?
When griefs around his pathway throng,
    Awake a helpful lay:

'Twill chase away the shadows drear,
    Make hearts forget their pain,
The list'ners will rejoice to hear
    The message of that strain.

Have you a word, a little word,
    For someone at your side?
'Tis sweeter than the song of bird
    To him when ills betide;

'Tis comfort in the hour of grief,
    It makes the burden light;
The wounded spirit finds relief,
    The clouded sky grows bright.

Have you a light, a little light,
    To cast a guiding ray?
Then let it shine with glory bright,
    Upon a pilgrim's way:

O sing your song for Christ to bless,
    And speak a word of cheer;
Your light will lead to happiness
    Some soul in pathways drear.

A. J. SHOWALTER, 1915

CLEANSING

CREATE IN ME A CLEAN HEART

I long to offer You a pure heart, O Lord. I seek to be worthy in Your presence. How can I be faultless in Your sight except by Your forgiveness? Forgive me and create in me a pure heart. Know my thoughts, my ways, my motives. Reveal my wrongs to me. By Your strength and my will, may they be removed. Help me forgive those who have hurt me, and help me forgive myself.

When all that separates me from You is removed, I lift my heart and hands to You in praise. Now I'm free from sin, anger, and resentment! I sense the presence of Your Holy Spirit. You are so close, I feel I can touch You. With all my being, I depend on You, Lord. With all my strength, I seek Your direction for me. With all my might, I strive to carry out Your calling. I will not allow doubts to creep in, lest I be tossed to and fro by the stormy ways of this world. I will come to You in faith; believing, knowing the answers in Your Bible are solid, strong, and true.

Thank You, Lord, for allowing me to approach You just as I am. Thank You for helping me confess my sins, for pleading my cause before my Father in heaven. How I praise You for hearing my prayers, for filling me with Your loving Holy Spirit and making my heart pure for You.

Create in me a pure heart, O God,
*   and renew a steadfast spirit within me.*
Do not cast me from your presence
*   or take your Holy Spirit from me.*
Restore to me the joy of your salvation
*   and grant me a willing spirit, to sustain me.*

PSALM 51:10–12 (NIV)

FIT FOR THE KING

Marcia gazed at her home with pride. She had worked all week preparing for this special evening. The kitchen sparkled. Everything was squeaky clean. The furniture shone so much one could almost see a reflection. The mantel and fireplace gave off a welcoming glow. Even the cupboards and closets were well organized. Marcia felt proud. A clean home meant a lot to her.

"It looks fit for a king," she said to herself. Soon she would prepare dinner for her friends from church.

The guests arrived. Dinner turned out great, without a hitch. To top it off, Marcia served strawberry shortcake and tea in the living room while they visited.

Marcia listened attentively as her friends told one

story after another of the wonderful things God had done for them. She became even more interested when they told the way God had cleansed their hearts and lives and how they were much happier since then.

Before she knew it, the evening came to a close. Hugs accompanied good-byes, and her friends were on their way. Marcia waved and smiled from the front steps as they backed out of the driveway; then she turned toward the front door.

She stepped back inside her lovely home and looked around. Marcia felt an emptiness deep within herself.

She was beginning to realize that her home sparkled with cleanliness, but God wanted to make her heart pure and spiritually fit for Him. Marcia knew He was asking to come into her life so she could experience the same wonderful love of God as her friends. She wondered where to start.

The couch before her cozy fireplace beckoned. Weariness set in as she snuggled at one end and wrapped herself in her afghan. Amber coals from the fireplace cast a soft glow. The living room stillness helped Marcia open her mind to what God was trying to show her.

She remembered her friends talking about the scripture, 1 John 1. She picked up her Bible and began reading about God's cleansing ways. Marcia realized that she had cleaned house for her guests, but she hadn't let God be the most honored guest of all. Now she wanted her life, as well as her home, fit for the King of kings.

"Dear, Lord, come into my life—," she began whispering.

> *If we claim to be without sin, we deceive ourselves and the truth is not in us. If we confess our sins, he is faithful and just and will forgive us our sins and purify us from all unrighteousness.*
>
> 1 JOHN 1:8–9 (NIV)

THE FEATHER DUSTER

Renee came home from college for winter break. Her first year of campus life had been a huge adjustment. College activities had made her busy during the past few months. She felt as if everything was being turned upside down. Church and Christian friends were set aside and replaced with studies, college events, and parties.

Sandpaper grated on Renee's soul. All of her

activities were good, but careless words and standards had crept into her way of life. Could it be her imagination, or was this abrasive feeling God quietly talking to her heart?

Renee looked forward to going home and being with her parents for a couple of weeks. She especially loved working with her father in his small-town store again. Renee and her dad had enjoyed many long talks while stocking and cleaning.

Once she arrived home, it didn't take long for Renee to plunge full-steam ahead into the store routine.

One night after they locked up, Renee stopped what she was doing and watched her father methodically clean. His movements swayed in rhythmic efficiency. Up the ladder, across the shelves of goods with his feather duster, he shuffled as he whistled "Take Time to Be Holy" and "Amazing Grace." God's familiar presence stirred within Renee.

"Dad," she sighed thoughtfully, "why do you take so much time to clean? Everything looks great. It's only a few particles of dust."

Her father continued maneuvering the feather duster through crooks and crannies. He stopped whistling and gazed down at his daughter. It seemed as though he saw past her question and knew her thoughts.

"Every corner must be clean, Renee. Otherwise the store wouldn't be its best. It requires care so it looks right and has a fresh, clean smell for everyone who comes in the door."

He waved his feather duster at Renee and smiled. "Our lives need God's constant cleaning and care, too, you know. Otherwise we can't be totally happy as His children, nor can God be entirely pleased with us."

Renee knew what she must do. She walked across the store to the household items and reached for a brand-new feather duster just like her father's worn one.

"Dad, I want to buy this and take it back to college. I plan to hang it by my door so I can remember what's most important in my Christian life."

Renee's father climbed down the ladder and gave his daughter a hug. "Honey, you can't buy that feather duster. You can have it."

Father and daughter returned to work cleaning the shelves, both with feather dusters in hand. A joyful whistling duet floated heavenward with one well-known hymn after another.

Search me, O God, and know my heart;
test me and know my anxious thoughts.
See if there is any offensive way in me,
and lead me in the way everlasting.

PSALM 139:23–24 (NIV)

TAKE TIME TO BE HOLY

Take time to be holy,
    Speak oft with your Lord;
Abide in Him always,
    And feed on His Word.
Make friends of God's children,
    Help those who are weak,
Forgetting in nothing
    His blessing to seek.

Take time to be holy,
    The world rushes on;
Spend much time in secret,
    With Jesus alone.
By looking to Jesus,
    Like Him thou shalt be;
Thy friends in thy conduct
    His likeness shall see.

Take time to be holy,
　　Let Him be thy guide;
And run not before Him,
　　Whatever betide.
In joy or in sorrow,
　　Still follow the Lord,
And, looking to Jesus,
　　Still trust in His Word.

Take time to be holy,
　　Be calm in thy soul,
Each thought and each motive
　　Beneath His control.
Thus led by His Spirit
　　To fountains of love,
Thou soon shalt be fitted
　　For service above.

WILLIAM DUNN LONGSTAFF, 1882

COMFORTING

YOUR COMFORTING PRESENCE

Thank You for being near during this time of suffering, Lord. Without You, it would be more than I could bear. Your comforting presence calms and strengthens me. I'm grateful for Your providing me short periods of relief so I can regain my bearings and fix my thoughts on You.

I don't see any purpose for my pain, Lord. I've pleaded for You to remove it from me, yet it still remains. The tears I shed in agony are beyond measure.

Why do You allow me to suffer like this? There must be a purpose. Even so, I will give You glory and praise for Your help to come. In spite of my distress, I will trust You with all my heart. I can't comprehend Your reasoning, but I will acknowledge Your directions for me. In spite of my anguish, I place my faith in You, Father. This tiny morsel of faith I have can only come from You. I place my hope in Your wisdom, Father.

Although I experience pain beyond description, You use this same pain to bring forth a harvest of righteousness so it can help others. Thank You, Lord, for giving me courage and strength to keep going.

Your Bible promises me that suffering produces perseverance; and as I persevere, You help me grow in character. Then as I grow in character, hope springs forth.

When I have no tangible hope, I still have confidence given by You, Lord. Thank You for Your comforting assurance. It may not appear logical or be easily understood. It's a deep, free-flowing confidence and joy, mixed together with the power of Your victorious Holy Spirit, that surpasses all human understanding!

When my strength ebbs to nothing, You lift me up. Your Son suffered and died so I could receive You as my Comforter. Thank You for giving me durability, hope for the future, and even life eternal.

Because I'm growing in You, I'm learning to let You use my sufferings, my weaknesses, and my hardships. Let even the insults and persecutions be used for Your glory. My hope is in You, Father. You have a marvelous way of transforming tragedies into triumphs so I can tell others the wondrous things You do.

Thank You for loving me through all this and not turning Your face from me when I don't handle things the best way. Thank You for hearing my cries for Your comfort and help. My hope is in You, Father, for You have promised when we sow in tears, we shall reap in joy.

Even though I grieve, I feel Your mercy and love. In spite of my suffering, I know I will experience glory with You in heaven some day. When I think of that glorious eternity, sufferings here do not compare.

Praise be to the God and Father of our Lord Jesus Christ, the Father of compassion and the God of all comfort, who comforts us in all our troubles, so that we can comfort those in any trouble with the comfort we ourselves have received from God.

2 CORINTHIANS 1:3–4 (NIV)

COMFORTING HANDS

Arla felt overwhelmed as she gazed at her mother's belongings. Everywhere she looked in the house she saw family treasures and mountains of paperwork. She dreaded having to go through it all.

It had only been a few days since her mother passed away. Arla felt forsaken and lost. She wondered where she could find any comfort.

Arla sat wearily on a box in the garage and prayed for help through trembling lips. "I can't do this on my own, Lord," she whispered.

Tears streamed down her cheeks, accompanied by muffled sobs. Until now, Arla hadn't been able to cry since her mother died. She continued praying for a long time, the tears washing and cleansing her wounded heart. Finally, she stopped. A presence known well to

Arla surrounded her: the comforting love of God.

Arla noticed the workbench. There lay her mother's gardening gloves and some small tools. Memories returned of the many hours when she had joined her mother in the flower garden. Her mom often handed her a tool and showed how working the soil and flowers with her hands could be a good way of sorting out life's problems. Arla remembered them working alongside each other, sharing secrets and concerns, later taking them to God in prayer. God had touched her mom with a special gift of gardening and listening.

Arla wondered if God was trying to comfort and help her in the same way now. Before she knew it, she gathered the bulbs and seeds her mom had left. She slipped on the gloves, carried the collection to the serene backyard, sank to her knees, and began digging.

She felt God's sweet comfort as she dug holes, planted bulbs, and dropped the seeds in place. Her thoughts cleared. Decisions Arla needed to make began falling into place. She knew she wasn't alone. She had the same wise, comforting God who had been with her mother and her all along.

Misunderstood

I can't believe this is happening, God. Why was I misunderstood? It hurts so much. I've lost confidence in myself. Can't I do anything right? This must be my fault. How could I have prevented such a terrible misunderstanding from happening, Lord? I know I must put my trust and confidence in You, but my heart is crushed. I tried to do good. Please forgive me, Lord, if I did wrong. Assist me in making things right.

It helps me when I read how You, Lord Jesus, were considered only a carpenter's son from Nazareth. You, perfect and holy, were misunderstood, falsely accused, and mistreated. Some thought nothing good could come from Nazareth.

I try to serve You, but my efforts seem in vain. I want to please You with all my heart. Sometimes, though, things become confused and misunderstood. This is when I'm bewildered.

I realize You were accused of blasphemy. Although innocent, still You loved everyone. You were beaten and hung on the cross like a common criminal for the sins of all. You even died for the same people who helped crucify You!

Thank You, Lord, for understanding me when I try to do right. You know my true intentions. In spite of my frustration and impatience, help me to keep trusting You. I know there are times we must share Your suffering.

When things go wrong, please help me not to act like a martyr with a self-righteous attitude. Remind me instead, Lord, to search my heart and see if there are any wrongful ways in me. Show me if my motives and actions aren't what they should be. Grant me strength, I pray, to go to others, admit my shortcomings, and ask forgiveness for where I went wrong. If my heart is pure, I pray for Your defense and aid. When others gossip and twist the truth about me, I will still trust in Your help.

When they were arresting You and taking You to the cross, You forgave us all without being asked. You never sinned or lied. You never answered back when insulted. You never threatened to retaliate. You never toiled endlessly at influencing others to take Your side against Your offenders. Help me not to stoop so low as to fall into these petty traps.

Heal my broken spirit. Comfort me, O Lord. Help me to forgive. Thank You already for how You are intervening for me and lifting all these problems to God, my Father.

A huge load lifts from me. I commit everything unconditionally to You. Because of all You do and teach me, a joy deeper than any ocean wells up within me. I will praise and trust in You.

Dear friends, do not be surprised at the painful trial you are suffering, as though something strange were happening to you. But rejoice that you participate in the sufferings of Christ, so that you may be overjoyed when his glory is revealed. If you are insulted because of the name of Christ, you are blessed, for the Spirit of glory and of God rests on you. If you suffer, it should not be as a murderer or thief or any other kind of criminal, or even as a meddler. However, if you suffer as a Christian, do not be ashamed, but praise God that you bear that name.

1 Peter 4:12–16 (niv)

Seeing the Whole Picture

Andrew and Claudia tremendously loved and enjoyed their three children, ages two through eleven. Evenings often included a wrestling match in the middle of the living room floor with two-year-old Nathaniel under a three-foot mountain of arms and legs.

Although Nathaniel was little, he kept up with his older siblings quite well. Nathaniel loved playing

Superman. When his parents weren't looking, the little boy often jumped from his dresser to the top bunk bed. They warned him repeatedly against these daring leaps, with little success.

One day Claudia heard a crash come from the bedroom, followed by Nathaniel's loud wail. She ran to his room and gathered Nathaniel in her arms. Claudia could never get a straight answer from Nathaniel about what happened, but he appeared to be fine.

A couple days later Claudia didn't like the color of Nathaniel's fingertips, so she took him to their long-standing family doctor. The exam showed a broken arm. Claudia felt terrible that she and Andrew hadn't recognized it before. The doctor comforted her, explaining his son's similar leg break had also gone unrecognized for a couple of days.

Claudia and her son were sent to X-ray, where the atmosphere was entirely different. Each question of how, when, or where Nathaniel's arm was broken couldn't be answered with certainty. Wrestling matches or Superman. Claudia wasn't sure. All she cared about was comforting her little boy.

Unspoken words, facial expressions, and attitudes accused Claudia of abusing her son.

Claudia and Nathaniel headed back to the doctor's office. Claudia felt angry and hurt. During the short moments in the elevator, she prayed for guidance and a gracious attitude.

When they returned to the doctor with the X-ray results in hand, Claudia told him about the critical demeanor of the technicians. She went on to explain that she wished they would have openly discussed their concern with her instead of being critical and judgmental. She had nothing to hide.

Nathaniel did well with his cast through the next few weeks. He soon discovered it gave great karate chops during the evening wrestling matches—a new thing for his parents to curb.

Before long, the active little boy mended nicely. Claudia took him back to the doctor for a recheck and follow-up X-rays.

This time the attitude of the technicians was cheerful and friendly. After all, they got more than the X-ray picture. The doctor had apparently helped them see the whole picture of an active, fun-filled, loving family.

Sometimes we are victims of misunderstandings. Innocent people often suffer.

We can be thankful as we ask God for help. He is able to comfort and intervene. We find the key is for us to trust God and maintain an attitude pleasing to Him.

And we know that all things work together for good to them that love God, to them who are the called according to his purpose.

ROMANS 8:28 (KJV)

THE LILY OF THE VALLEY

I have found a friend in Jesus,
He's everything to me,
He's the fairest of ten thousand to my soul;
The Lily of the Valley,
In Him alone I see
All I need to cleanse and make me fully whole.
In sorrow He's my comfort,
In trouble He's my stay;
He tells me every care on Him to roll.
He's the Lily of the Valley,
The Bright and Morning Star,
He's the fairest of ten thousand to my soul.

CHARLES W. FRY, 1881

CORRECTING

THANK YOU FOR PRUNING ME

Thank You for pruning me, Father, when I become lax in following You. Sometimes I look in the mirror and see only a small amount of Your spiritual fruit being produced in me, and I'm not happy. Thank You for stepping in and helping me change.

Your correcting presence isn't always easy. In fact, sometimes, Father, it is downright painful. I still thank You for the outcome.

I praise You for revealing my shortcomings and providing me with Your lessons, for helping me listen more to You. I'm grateful for Your presence. Thank You for how You guide me through Your Word so I can grow and produce good fruit in Your Spirit.

Each time You need to prune me, Lord, I will remember how much You care for me.

Search me, O God, and know my heart;
*   test me and know my anxious thoughts.*
See if there is any offensive way in me,
*   and lead me in the way everlasting.*
                                        PSALM 139:23–24 (NIV)

Teach me to do your will,
  for you are my God;
may your good Spirit
  lead me on level ground.

PSALM 143:10 (NIV)

I will exalt you, my God the King;
  I will praise your name for ever and ever.

PSALM 145:1 (NIV)

STIRRING THE CONSCIENCE

Charles always looked forward to his walks through
the woods near his home. Today was no exception. The
crisp fall air stung his cheeks as he shuffled through dry,
multicolored leaves along the trail.

Things were stressful. He couldn't put his finger
on what was troubling him. Fortunately, Charles found
relaxation and peace on his walk. He thought of the
people he had contacted lately about issues he didn't
like at work. Should he have gone directly to those in
charge instead of stirring up things with his coworkers?
Was his point of view really correct, or did he give
what he said a convenient twist to add impact? *After*

all, he thought, *what's so bad about a little white lie?*

Charles trudged on. The gurgling creek he jumped over laughed a cheerful greeting. Even with the cold weather, it hadn't frozen. A little further on, Charles noticed the small, quiet pond. Ice was forming over its surface. The pond's water was always stagnant. He pressed on its already unyielding surface and thought of the dead mire beneath that would lazily gather bugs and impurities next summer.

People trusted Charles for his word because he proclaimed Christianity. His conscience prodded him about the gossip he had started. Charles shoved the guilt from his mind.

The crisp air grew colder. Charles raised his collar and picked up his pace. He prepared to jump the stream on his return home. Instead, he stopped short. This time he couldn't ignore his conscience. Charles saw a true Christian's life to be like the clear bubbling stream—clean, open. He stooped down and stirred it with his forefinger. The water gently yielded and swirled around his hand.

Charles knew the pond's layer of ice would thicken more every day. He thought again about the murky water.

Charles seated himself on a nearby log. He felt stunned as his conscience helped him realize he, also, was freezing out God's guiding presence more every day. God ministered to him. Charles knew he had to make things right with those he had gossiped to and about.

"Forgive me, Lord," he whispered. "Help others to forgive me. I pray for Your strength and for a good conscience, so that I will never act like this again. And thank You, Lord, for whispering to me with Your still, small voice."

"I strive always to keep my conscience clear before God and man."

ACTS 24:16 (NIV)

I'M LEARNING TO OBEY YOU

Whenever I have the good sense to obey You, Lord, I find more reasons to love You. When I trust You with my goals and dreams, things fall into place. A strange yet wonderful harmony fills my heart. There is no way I wish to go back on my commitment of serving and obeying You as my God. I huddle daily under Your protective canopy. Your mighty power surrounds me, keeping me from sin and harm. To You, my Lord, I give all the praise.

I don't even question that I am Your child. I know You love me, Lord; and I belong to You. How much I love You in return! Each day I long to do the things You ask of me. Because of Your love, I'm learning how to obey You more. Thank You for assuring me that You and my Father in heaven know what is best for me. I want to remain close to You, Lord, to shun sin and do what is right in Your eyes. When I slip, I'm so glad You still love me as Your child. When things go wrong, You gather me up and set me safely back on the right path.

I can't obey You with just my own power. Only through the strength You place within me can I succeed. As I walk daily with You, my love for You matures and grows stronger. I thrive on Your wonderful presence. I look forward to seeing You and my Father in heaven face-to-face without being ashamed. Thank You, Lord!

"If any man serve me, let him follow me; and where I am, there shall also my servant be: if any man serve me, him will my Father honour."

JOHN 12:26 (KJV)

A BEAUTIFUL CHARACTER

Holiness is beauty. There is no beauty like that of a pure character. The grandest sight on this earth is not the march of the all-conquering storm whose cloudy battalions go rushing through the sounding heavens; the most beautiful thing on earth is not the garden which opens, and sends forth from its censers fragrance; the beauty of the soul lies in its secret chambers; and the rich, deep, just, holy and loving natures—these are the beautiful things of this world. There is nothing so beautiful as Christ in man.

HENRY WARD BEECHER

GOD'S PROVISION
FOR STRENGTH

When we think we have learned all of life's lessons, and our answers are pat and sure, God has a way of exposing our weaknesses and limitations. Our shortcomings stare us bluntly in the face. We gaze at them and are often frustrated. It isn't long, though, until we learn to realize who really is all-knowing, all-righteous. Certainly not us.

When we yield to His careful chastising, one by one He prunes the useless obstacles that have sapped our strength and wisdom. The process is often slow and painful. Other times, He even adds a little humor to the process.

Either way, God brings us through with victory and triumph. Through Him, our strength mounts up as the eagle soars; our wisdom increases in holy humility. In due time, we see the reasoning of it all and give Him praise for His pruning, wisdom, and grace. Let's thank God not only during our smooth experiences, but also while we wince and yield to His spiritual pruning.

He loves us enough to correct and make us into Christians after His own heart. After the pruning, new growth in character, remarkable strength, and abundant joy burst forth!

HAVE THINE OWN WAY, LORD

Have Thine own way, Lord!
Have Thine own way!
Thou art the Potter, I am the clay.
Mold me and make me after Thy will,
While I am waiting, yielded and still.

Have Thine own way, Lord!
Have Thine own way!
Search me and try me, Master, today!
Whiter than snow, Lord, wash me just now,
As in Thy presence humbly I bow.

Have Thine own way, Lord!
Have Thine own way!
Wounded and weary, help me, I pray!
Power, all power, surely is Thine!
Touch me and heal me, Savior divine.

Have Thine own way, Lord!
Have Thine own way!
Hold o'er my being absolute sway!
Fill with Thy Spirit till all shall see
Christ only, always, living in me.

ADELAIDE ADDISON POLLARD, 1907

CREATING

YOUR CREATING PRESENCE

I praise You, O my Lord.
      From the innermost part of my soul,
I will bless Your holy name.
      I praise You, O my Lord.
You are lofty and noble. You are surrounded
      with brilliance and supreme greatness.
A robe of pure light wraps around You.

I praise You, O my Lord,
      for Your magnificent creation.
I thank You and will not forget the wonderful
      things You have made for my enjoyment.

You spread out the heavens
      like an enormous canopy.
You cause the clouds to ride on wings of wind.
You whisper and they release their burden
      of rain to the earth below.

You speak. The thunder rolls!
      The lightning cracks!
Your hand scoops out the oceans
      and sets boundaries for their water.

Your finger guides the rivers
    over mountains and down through valleys,
    where they trickle into springs, lakes, and
    ponds.

Animals, large and small,
    find their way to drink.
Birds nest nearby.
You provide us all with
    Your life-giving liquid substance.
You raise Your hand slightly
    and cause the grass, trees,
    and flowers to grow.
You open Your hand and meet our needs.

I praise You, O my Lord, for Your love.
It goes beyond the heavens and pierces deep
    into the earth, reaching all who love You.
Your love embraces the entire earth, from the
    east to the west.

I praise You, O my Lord, as you nourish and
    care for everything You have created.
You show more compassion than a loving
    father or mother.

You know every part of our beings,
    our physical makeup, every hair, our
    emotions and innermost thoughts.
You know it all.

Through storms and seasons,
Your Spirit restores and heals.
You seek out and save that which is lost.

I praise You, O my Lord,
    with my thoughts and actions.
Help me, I pray, so I can be mindful
    and take care of all You have given me.
I praise You, O my Lord;
    To all who love and trust in You, Lord,
You are everlasting to everlasting.

GOLDIE'S FRUIT

Most of the time we visualize teenagers being interested in dating, cars, music, and food. Although this was true of a church youth group in Plains, Montana, their interests went much further.

    This group had a very special leader. Goldie was

her name. Having never married, she was able to invest unlimited hours and energy on the future leaders of God's church.

Goldie had a marvelous way of collecting the group to go huckleberry picking in the hills or swimming in a local quiet spot of a river. She showed them how to take everyday wild plants most people thought were weeds and make them into a salad or side vegetable.

Goldie helped her youth appreciate creation and remember the One who made it all. She took them on hikes and to retreats and camps. She gathered them around campfires where they could share their feelings, sing, and pray together.

A favorite place the youth liked was a small waterfall not far from town. The water rippled joyfully as one testimony after another burst forth.

Goldie never said a lot. She listened and set a good Christian example. Her love and prayers for the youth extended far beyond her years.

Goldie has gone to be with the Lord now but she has left memories of a vibrant, enthusiastic youth group that she taught through the simple things of God's creation.

The fruit of Goldie's labor continues. Many whom she influenced are now in active service for the Lord. They range from ministers to faithful laypeople. Now they are the ones who are passing on her lessons, listening, and caring like their beloved youth leader did.

I thank God for the fruit that comes from the Goldies in this world and how they touch our lives.

DID YOU KNOW—?

Did you know about these miracles of God's creation?

The hummingbird has an egg smaller than a pencil eraser. Its nest is no larger than a marshmallow. Its delicate wings have one free-moving joint, so they are stiff. It can tilt its wings and fly up and down as well as forward and backward. Its tiny wings can flap thirty-five times a second!

The song sparrow is only five inches long. It always sings. Its lovely trill can be heard in even the hottest part of the day. It masters songs learned from its parents at an early age. Young sparrows learn to follow their parents from birth. Their natural way of imprinting enables the little ones to always recognize the call most important to them: that of their parents.

The deer must step to the edge of a woods in order to find food, where more sunlight stimulates plant growth. To protect the deer, God created it with four compartments in its stomach. This way it can eat as fast as it can swallow and fill its "paunch" (the first compartment). Later, in a safer area, the deer can chew, regurgitate, and rechew its food three more times so every ounce of nutrition is extracted.

A blue whale begins in its mother's womb as a tiny egg. Shortly after it is born, it grows to almost 30 tons. Its daily meals include nine thousand pounds of sea creature morsels. When free, the blue whale swims an average of one hundred miles per day. It can grow to one hundred feet and weigh 150 tons!

A mountain is bigger than hundreds of millions of whales. All of our mountains combined are a dot on our earth. The sun is one hundred million times larger than Earth. From over ninety-six million miles away, it can give us a sunburn. There are stars millions of times bigger than Earth. Billions of those stars are a part of the ultra-gigantic, powerful, swirling, cloudy Milky Way. Billions of galaxies fill the universe!

God is bigger and more powerful than any of this. He created everything with perfect timing and synchronization. Not only does God care for this vast creation, but he watches out for each one of us.

He created us in His own image. He longs to imprint His voice in our minds and hearts so we will always know and follow Him.

Let them praise the name of the LORD:
for he commanded, and they were created.
He hath also stablished them for ever and ever;
he hath made a decree which shall not pass.
Praise the LORD from the earth. . .
Fire, and hail; snow, and vapour;
stormy wind fulfilling his word:
Mountains, and all hills;
fruitful trees, and all cedars:
Beasts, and all cattle;
creeping things, and flying fowl:
Kings of the earth, and all people;
princes, and all judges of the earth:
Both young men, and maidens;
old men, and children:
Let them praise the name of the LORD:
for his name alone is excellent;
his glory is above the earth and heaven.
. . .Praise ye the LORD.

PSALM 148:5–14 (KJV)

ENCOURAGING

YOUR ENCOURAGING PRESENCE

Concerns piled up around me. I felt tired, frustrated, and discouraged. At my wit's end, I called on Your help. I poured out each worry to You and felt Your attentive, encouraging presence. You comforted my soul. A peaceful feeling of Your reassurance swept over me. Perhaps someone was praying for me at that moment. Could it have been so?

I've always tried to be the strong one, Lord, one other people could lean upon. I didn't want to burden anyone with my cares. Only You know my needs.

I was pleased and surprised when I received an encouraging note from a faithful prayer warrior, assuring me that I wasn't alone. Did You place my needs upon her heart to pray for me? If so, thank You, Lord.

Thank You for the different ways You surround me with Your encouraging presence and my caring friends.

Humble yourselves, therefore, under God's mighty hand, that he may lift you up in due time. Cast all your anxiety on him because he cares for you.

1 PETER 5:6–7 (NIV)

FULL-CIRCLE ENCOURAGEMENT

In my recent book, *When I'm Praising God*, I wrote about a teenage girl named Michelle. The story, "A Rare Jewel," shares Michelle's faithfulness and undying love for the Lord and for children.

When the book came out, I read the tribute about her aloud in our morning church service. Then I called Michelle to the front and presented her with a copy of the book. It was a very touching moment. Hugs were exchanged. Tears were shed.

Months passed. Various circumstances caused me to feel overworked and unappreciated. I'm sure weariness and self-pity played a large part in how I felt. The problems I struggled with, however, were serious. I brought my needs to the Lord and asked for His encouraging presence and strength.

During the time of my struggle, I had no idea that Michelle would be the answer to my prayer. Her pre-college English teacher asked the class to write something about their most memorable experience. Michelle prepared her story well.

Here are excerpts of what she wrote:

My peak experience happened recently at church. I have been an assistant teacher in a Sunday school class at our church for the past three years. I worked with a very special woman trying to build an exquisite children's program. Anita and I have become great friends and coworkers over the years.

On this particular Sunday, I felt down and out. All of a sudden I heard her announce my name to the entire congregation. She was dedicating her book to all the wonderful people in her life: One of them was me! To even further my surprise, she had written about me in her book, telling the world I was a 'Rare Jewel.' I was so amazed that I cried.

I still get teary-eyed thinking about how much this lady means to me, and I to her. Someday, I hope to make her proud of me by fulfilling my desires to be a youth leader.

This was the best experience of my life, and it will never be forgotten.

Excerpt used by permission from
MICHELLE WILSON

Shortly after, Bob and I had dinner at Michelle and her family's home. Michelle told me about how her teacher read her paper. He appeared overwhelmed, and the class was speechless. Some even broke down and cried. Michelle's story penetrated the hearts of many that day.

I believe I received the biggest blessing. It was the answer to my pitiful prayer, asking God for encouragement and strength. God touched us both when He brought His encouraging blessing full circle.

I KNOW WHAT YOU THINK OF ME

Thank You for loving me in every instance of my life, Lord. I know what You think of me. Without a shadow of doubt, I'm confident You love me for my insecurities as well as my talents.

I used to feel I constantly had to go about doing good for others in order to win Your love and approval. In the same way, I felt the need to overachieve so I could gain appreciation and praise from my friends and loved ones. I was convinced no one would like me if I slipped up in the least. I had to be absolutely perfect all the time or I would lose Your love for me and the love of others, as well.

I don't know if I was putting myself on a teetering pedestal, or if I simply felt unworthy of Your love or everyone else's. Either way, You took my insecurities and replaced them with assurance of Your unwavering care and devotion. Thank You, dear Lord, for Your merciful kindness.

How I praise You for showing me over and over again that You love me in all situations. I feel tremendous relief for Your teaching me from Your word that Your strength shows up all the more in my weaknesses.

Thank You, Lord, for loving me at all times. Thank You for Your constant compassion and forgiveness when I'm not perfect.

When my children learned to walk, they took a few steps and fell. I never scolded them for falling, but praised them for the steps they took. You know my heart and my love for You. I know what You think of me, when You remind me to rest in You. Thank You for helping me to stop trying to constantly gain approval from others and You. I can't be perfect in everything. Only You are perfect.

Your grace and understanding are so wonderful, Lord. Thank You for how You reach out with Your hand and help me when I'm stumbling and weary. You are my One, true God. Although I'll keep trying to do my best in everything, I will not make perfectionism my god. You have not saved me by any good I do, but by Your grace.

I praise You, Lord, that I don't have to try to impress You. Although I'm not perfect, I love You with all my heart. Thank You for loving me just the way I am.

NEVER GOOD ENOUGH

Andrea gave her first-grade classroom a quick glance. Everything appeared perfectly in place, ready for the first day of school. Soon the children would arrive. Although the room looked top-notch to parents and fellow teachers, Andrea could see flaws. School hadn't started, and she was already exhausted. She had arrived at school before anyone else, including the principal and secretary.

Andrea thought back over her weekend. She'd spent hours doing little things here and there for people. In spite of all her well-meaning duties, Andrea's husband, Patrick, and her family complained she didn't have enough time for them.

Andrea sighed even thinking about it. "I'm stretched so thin trying to do for others, Lord, but no one seems to appreciate me," she murmured. "I guess I can never be good enough."

Several weeks of school sped by. Andrea's schedule became crazier than ever. On top of everything else, she was now trying to be all things to all her students.

Six-year-old Kelsie especially worried Andrea. The little girl reminded Andrea of what she had been like as a child.

One morning before class Andrea discussed the girl's situation with a Christian friend who taught down the hall. "If Kelsie doesn't change and quit stressing herself out, she's going to snap." Andrea went on thoughtfully. "She acts as if the only way anyone will approve of her is for her to do everything perfectly."

The other teacher looked at Andrea with a knowing smile. "Is that Kelsie you're talking about, or you?"

Andrea was speechless. A slap in the face couldn't have hit her harder.

That evening she told Patrick what her friend had said. Andrea began realizing she didn't love herself very much, so she felt no one else did, either. After many hours of talking and spending time in prayer, Patrick helped Andrea accept God's unconditional love and love from him and her family.

Andrea's anxiousness melted away. She was finally

able to relax and let go of the imperfections. For the first time ever, she realized her family, friends, and especially God, loved Andrea for herself. She was no longer a woman or little girl who felt inadequate. New joy and closeness grew in her family relationship because she could finally enjoy them instead of always trying to be everything for them. Andrea found a new life of happiness and also a greater understanding of Kelsie's needs. She thanked God for the freedom He gave, where she could lean on His perfect example.

By day the LORD directs his love,
at night his song is with me—
a prayer to the God of my life.

PSALM 42:8 (NIV)

HIS EYE IS ON THE SPARROW

Why should I feel discouraged,
    Why should the shadows come,
Why should my heart be lonely,
    And long for heaven and home,
When Jesus is my portion?
    My constant friend is He:
His eye is on the sparrow,
    And I know He watches me.

"Let not your heart be troubled,"
    His tender word I hear,
And resting on His goodness.
    I lose my doubt and fears;
Though by the path He leadeth,
    But one step I may see;
His eye is on the sparrow,
    And I know He watches me.

Whenever I am tempted,
　　Whenever clouds arise,
When songs give place to sighing,
　　When hope within me dies,
I draw the closer to Him,
　　From care He sets me free;
His eye is on the sparrow,
　　And I know He watches me.

CIVILLA D. MARTIN, 1905

FAITHFUL

Hands-Off Faith

Thank You for teaching me to trust You, Lord. Trust is nearly an unknown word in this world. Having complete faith in You is my most difficult spiritual challenge.

Because of the teachings in Your Word and Your constant nudging, I'm learning to trust You more. By believing in You with all my heart and soul, You show me the way.

By taking my concerns to You, I find wise answers. Unfortunately, there are times when my impatient "fix-it" nature slips into action, and I try helping You along a little.

Help You? The Creator, the controller of the universe? I don't help. I muddle things up and manage to be in the way! Forgive me, Lord.

Now I'm learning to have faith in my prayers and trust You unconditionally in all things. Thank You for helping me to slowly, painfully grow in my understanding of how powerful a hands-off faith really can be. When I stay out of the way and allow You to work, I can stand back and watch Your miracles happen!

You not only teach me to trust, You help me become trustworthy. You show me how stepping in, manipulating, and "fixing things" are a lack of trust and are displeasing to You.

How I praise You for Your glorious works. How wonderful it is when I do trust You with all my heart. How grateful I am for Your directing my paths into truth and righteousness. You bring me peace.

Lord, I offer You my trust in this situation. I take my hands off and leave everything in Yours. I praise You already for Your wise insight.

The next time I feel anxious and want to do something about a problem, please strongly remind me to stop before I take action. The something I must do is get on my knees and pray so You can provide the best answers.

Trust in the LORD with all your heart
and lean not on your own understanding;
in all your ways acknowledge him,
and he will make your paths straight.

PROVERBS 3:5–6 (NIV)

PLANTERS AND GARDENERS

The first time I walked into the little church, I was only eighteen years old. The people were the friendliest group I had ever met. They made me feel like they cared about me.

The service began with a teenager playing the piano. The music added to a reverent worship service. It came time for the pastor to speak. His sermon was simple. His speech faltered, yet his message touched my heart. It wasn't what he said, but his attitude that meant the most to me.

I kept returning to the church. It became my home away from home. I fell in love with the people. The pastor kept saying that being a Christian was not enough. We needed to become dedicated Christians.

After much thought, I fell to my knees alone by my bed and rededicated my heart to the Lord. My life changed to a wonderful adventure in Him.

My pastor and his wife were always there for me and for the other members of our church youth group. They taught us how to grow spiritually and emotionally. They helped us develop our skills by showing us how to lead music, teach children, sing special songs, and conduct an entire worship service. They even allowed me to be one of the speakers. What a scary, awesome experience!

Now, Bob and I are passing our knowledge on to our young people and helping them develop into the church of tomorrow.

Thank you, Pastor Buz and Shirley Miller and other faithful Christians in the church, for planting spiritual seedlings in our youth. Thank you for gardening us to become effective church leaders of today.

Your Faithful Servants

Thank You, Father, for Your faithful servants who bless our lives. Thank You for supplying their needs and surrounding us with Your blessed presence.

Reaping the Harvest

The husband and wife team accepted the job of being our youth leaders. They plunged in with enthusiastic vigor. Their son, Bob, became youth president, and I, vice president. We spent hours singing around the piano with our young pianist (who is still playing in church today).

We had a lot of fun, but our youth leaders also taught what it meant to be faithful Christians. Not so much with speeches, but more by their example.

One time the husband gave a lesson in our youth meeting on how our lights must shine steadily for Jesus, not just off and on. He used the example of blinking and steady lights, helping us see through the darkness. In the same way, finding God's presence is much easier for someone who watches a steady, faithful Christian. I'll never forget that story.

They always kept their home open to us. We had parties with popcorn, homemade ice cream, and lots of fun. We did car washes and went to citywide "sing-spirations," and we all went to camp meeting.

The time came for me to step into an adult world. I became Bob's wife. The youth leader (also a minister) performed our wedding ceremony. He and his wife became my father- and mother-in-law.

After much prayer, they kissed us good-bye. Bob and I went off to Bible college to study for the ministry.

Thank you, Mom and Dad, for tending and gardening us in our earlier years and for reaping a harvest of dedicated church leaders.

KEEPING MY WORD

I said I would be there to help out, Lord, but I'm tired. I don't feel like doing anything except snuggling in my chair and reading a good book. You have reminded me, though, to keep my word and not let others down. A promise is a promise is a promise. Forgive me, dear Lord, for even considering breaking my word.

I'm glad I followed through and kept my promise, Lord. Their smiles and gratitude made it all worthwhile. Thank You for Your guiding strength.

Hear my cry, O God;
listen to my prayer.
From the ends of the earth I call to you,
I call as my heart grows faint;
lead me to the rock that is higher than I.

I long to dwell in your tent forever
and take refuge in the shelter of your wings.
For you have heard my vows, O God;
you have given me the heritage of
those who fear your name.

Then will I ever sing praise to your name
and fulfill my vows day after day.
PSALM 61:1–2, 4–5, 8 (NIV)

FAITHFUL AND GENTLE NUDGE

A two-foot Westminster chime clock hangs on our living room wall. Its chimes fill our home with music and grace. The words to the chimes come from a phrase in *Handel's Messiah*.

Its faithful words say, "I know that my Redeemer liveth."

If I wind our clock once a week, make sure the hands are set correctly, and do nothing more, the clock will not work. In order to make the hands move forward, I must make one more small effort. I must give the pendulum a gentle touch with my finger to start its sway. It will then faithfully keep perfect time and chime out every quarter hour without fail until the following week. The time comes again where it requires another gentle nudge.

The same happens when we lead others to Christ. New life begins at that first moment of decision. Yet they are babies in the Lord. If we go off and leave them alone after they have accepted Christ, they may remain the same and not grow or may forget to keep God first in their lives.

What new Christians need is tender care and gentle nudges to their spiritual pendulums, reminding them how wonderful God is and how much there is to be thankful for: Jesus truly does love us and lives in our hearts.

Care and faithfulness flourish through care and faithfulness given.

Great Is Thy Faithfulness

Great is Thy faithfulness, O God my Father;
There is no shadow of turning with Thee;
Thou changest not, Thy compassions, they fail not;
As Thou hast been, Thou forever wilt be.

Summer and winter and springtime and harvest,
Sun, moon and stars in their courses above
Join with all nature in manifold witness
To Thy great faithfulness, mercy and love.

Pardon for sin and a peace that endureth
Thine own dear presence to cheer and to guide;
Strength for today and bright hope for tomorrow,
Blessings all mine, with ten thousand beside!

Great is Thy faithfulness!
Great is Thy faithfulness!
Morning by morning new mercies I see.
All I have needed Thy hand hath provided;
Great is Thy faithfulness, Lord, unto me!

THOMAS O. CHISHOLM, 1923

FORGIVING

YOUR FORGIVING PRESENCE

Here I am, Lord. I messed up again. I disappointed others, myself, and worst of all, You. The more I struggle with the lessons You teach me, the more I fall short. How can You possibly forgive me when I fail You so many times?

No matter how hard I try, I can't right all my wrongs. You remind me to ask in Your name, then You forgive me, once again.

Thank You for Your pardon. Your goodness and mercy go beyond my comprehension. I'm overwhelmed at the way You shower Your grace upon me. I simply don't understand how You love me so.

When I think of how I fall short, I marvel at all the times You forgive me. You remove my sinful stains and make me whiter than snow.

Your word tells me all I need to do is ask, then receive Your forgiveness. Is it true that all my sins are gone as far as the east is from the west, buried in the deepest sea? I can't grasp it all. I know well the presence of Your forgiving Holy Spirit and the calm, affirming love You give. Perhaps I don't have to completely understand. All I need to do is open my heart to You, repent of my sins, and accept Your mercy and forgiveness.

I do this right now in faith, believing. Strange. I feel a tremendous relief. Because I know You forgive me, a huge load lifts from my shoulders.

Thank You, Lord Jesus, for Your forgiving love and presence.

TEACH ME HOW TO FORGIVE

How can I forgive those who are repeatedly unkind to me? Don't they know they hurt me? Don't they care? I tried to work things out, with no success. I'm angry and confused, Lord. No matter how hard I try, I can't change my attitude. Please help me.

Although things aren't right, I still must learn to forgive others as You forgive me. I realize if I don't forgive, my unforgiveness will destroy me spiritually like a deadly cancer. I don't want my anger and bitterness to come between You and me.

When the Bible says I must forgive seventy-times-seven, does that mean I can keep track? I guess not. Forgiving doesn't mean maintaining a record or holding on to the past.

Teach me how to forgive, Lord. Please change my heart. Help me let go of the hurts. I know as long as

I hold on to them, I'm not really giving them all to You and forgiving. Heal my hurts, I pray. I don't have the strength to do this on my own. Fill me with Your forgiving presence. The ability to forgive the ones who hurt me can only come from You.

Let me not seek revenge or gloat if ill should befall those who mistreat me. Instead, help me to pray for their hearts to become submissive to Your ways. After this, let me leave the rest in Your hands.

When I hear twisted stories about me, calm me so I don't strike back with angry words. Grant me a gracious spirit. Help me forgive and continue praying. Along with this, please defend my honor when I am right; help me repent when I am wrong. The main One I must please is You, my Savior.

Lord, I know I've done my best, now. I leave everything in Your hands. Go before and behind me, I pray. Surround and fill me with Your power and unconditional, forgiving love.

Through all this, I give You glory and honor. All the past and future I forgive and commit to You.

In Jesus' name, amen.

Do not repay anyone evil for evil.
Be careful to do what is right in the eyes of
everybody. If it is possible, as far as it depends
on you, live at peace with everyone. Do not take
revenge, my friends, but leave room for God's
wrath, for it is written: "It is mine to avenge; I will
repay," says the Lord. On the contrary:

"If your enemy is hungry, feed him; if he is
thirsty, give him something to drink. In doing this,
you will heap burning coals on his head."
Do not be overcome by evil, but overcome evil
with good.

ROMANS 12:17–21 (NIV)

TWICE FORGIVEN

Jeff crumpled the list of monthly bills he had been working on for hours. He could pay most of them, but the medical expenses were way beyond his means.

Why did all this have to happen? Jeff slumped over his desk and clutched his hair with both hands. His wife, Cindy, rested quietly in the other room. Jeff felt thankful that the doctors were able to remove all the cancer, but Cindy would still lose several months' work and their needed income.

"Lord, I can never forgive Dad for not calling or even showing up at the hospital. Where is he when I need him the most?" Jeff muttered.

Jeff hurried the payments to the post office. One included a small token he had faithfully sent every month toward the huge medical bill and a promise to send more next month. He had to get back home to prepare a nice lunch for Cindy. How he loved her.

After lunch, Jeff and Cindy heard the mail carrier arrive. Jeff gathered the mail apprehensively. An envelope from the medical center fell to the floor. Jeff's heart sank. He gathered it up and opened it gingerly. It was from the accounts receivable department. It read:

"Because Cindy's expenses were all incurred

here at the medical center, we were able to combine invoices from the physicians, surgical department, lab, radiology, and her hospital fees into a lump sum. We are aware of how you have tried faithfully to pay this tremendous expense.

"A new fund has been introduced to our medical center called the Seventy-Times-Seven Fund. After reviewing your records, we're able to inform you that your bill has been erased.

"Our best wishes and prayers for Cindy's complete recovery."

Jeff dropped to the couch by his wife. "They forgave us the entire bill," he stammered.

Cindy took his hand and gave a squeeze.

"Let's pray and thank God," she whispered.

After they prayed, Jeff felt a deep sense of guilt. How could he be forgiven if he didn't forgive one of the dearest people in his life, his dad? Cindy smiled and nodded toward the phone. Jeff picked up the receiver and dialed.

"Dad? It's Jeff."

Jeff's resentments melted away. He waited with an open heart. Sobs came from the other end of the line. His father explained how he simply couldn't handle being at the hospital around all that was involved. Over and over he said how sorry he was. Jeff's father went on to tell how worried he had been but was too embarrassed to even call.

"It's okay, Dad, I forgive you. Cindy and I both love you. Cindy's doing fine." He cleared his throat. "By the way, what are you doing for dinner tonight?"

TALK WITH US, LORD, THYSELF REVEAL

Talk with us, Lord, Thyself reveal,
　　While here o'er earth we rove;
Speak to our hearts, and let us feel
　　The kindling of Thy love.

With Thee conversing, we forget
　　All time and toil and care;
Labor is rest, and pain is sweet,
　　If Thou, My God, art here.

Thou callest me to seek Thy face;
　　'Tis all I wish to seek;
To attend the whispers of Thy grace,
　　And hear Thee only speak.

Let this my every hour employ,
    Till I Thy glory see;
Enter into my Master's joy,
    And find my heaven in Thee.
Amen.

CHARLES WESLEY, 1740

FORGIVE AND FORGET

If I forgive, I must forget.
    Or forgive, I never shall do.
Forgiveness is like an unpaid bill
    Marked "paid," then torn in two.

No matter the fault, the debt is gone.
    I never shall see it again.
Instead, I behold the old rugged cross,
    Where Jesus forgave my sin.

FRIENDSHIP

YOUR FRIENDSHIP

Here I am, Lord, after the late shift. Work was hard, fast, and stressful. I'm tired, but my body is so tense I can't sleep. All I can think of is the quiet peace You give me. Thank You, God, for meeting me here in my weariness and for Your friendship.

Your sweet presence fills the air. A feeling of expectancy greets me, as though You have been waiting for me to share my work events with You. I sense You listening intently to my every concern. The victories, the crises, even the funny happenings. I also bring my coworkers to You in prayer.

Like a new chapter in a book, I feel You speak to me. You comfort and assure me of answers to my prayers.

Thank You for my loved ones sleeping in nearby rooms. Their soft, steady breathing sounds so good. I ask Your blessings on each one and thank You for keeping them safe.

My eyelids grow heavy; I find it difficult to form my thoughts on You.

"Rest, my beloved," I feel You say.

Thank You, Lord, for meeting me here again and being my dearest Friend.

LATE NIGHT MEETING

Late hours and fast pace frequently made Nancy's profession increasingly stressful and troublesome. This night was more exhausting than most. Nancy glanced at the clock. One hour to go until she could finally return home.

In the back of her mind, she knew where she wanted to be. Nancy looked forward to her time alone with God. Just Him, herself, and the calm.

Nancy wheeled into the driveway. Home at last. Her throbbing feet stumbled to the door. While she turned the key in the lock, Nancy became aware of a silvery moon's reflection. She turned and stared. How it shone in all its white splendor, as though it was lighting her way.

Nancy crept in silently so she wouldn't wake her family. Her body ached for sleep, but she was too filled with strain to even try. She paused for a moment and listened to the soft, even breathing coming from the bedrooms. Even the dog lay quietly. He knew it was Nancy. No bother.

She sank into a chair near the window and carefully pulled open the curtain. Faint morning shadows played across the yard. By now the birds twittered from nearby trees. A wild rabbit gingerly bounced from bush to bush.

It glanced up at the window, paid Nancy no heed, and went on with its morning rounds.

Silence. Pure tranquillity. Nancy pushed the window open and felt the chilly air caress her face. She could feel God's presence as though He had been waiting up for her like a faithful friend.

Little by little she shared her experiences with God. She complained and worried, laughed and cried, telling Him of each circumstance, asking for guidance. Finally, she thanked Him for carrying her through another night and keeping her safe.

Nancy leaned back and began reading her Bible. She listened while God tended her needs and advised her through His Word.

She brought her family and friends to His late-night throne, thanking and praising Him for past answers to prayers. She placed each of her beloved ones' needs before God and released them to His care.

Her body relaxed; her eyelids grew heavy.

"Rest, my beloved," she felt Him say.

Nancy creaked to her feet, gently closed the window, and shuffled toward a comfortable, welcoming bed.

"Thank You for meeting me here, Lord," she whispered back.

"These things I have spoken to you while being present with you. But the Helper, the Holy Spirit, whom the Father will send in My name, He will teach you all things, and bring to your remembrance all things that I said to you. Peace I leave with you, My peace I give to you; not as the world gives do I give to you. Let not your heart be troubled, neither let it be afraid."

JOHN 14:25–27 (NKJV)

"I am the true vine, and My Father is the vinedresser."
"Abide in Me, and I in you."
"As the Father loved Me, I also have loved you; abide in My love."

JOHN 15:1, 4, 9 (NKJV)

YOU SATISFY MY SOUL

Heavenly Father, thank You for being so kind to me and for being my dearest Friend. When I cry out and search for You, my God, You are here. When my parched soul thirsts for You during the droughts, You fill me to overflowing with living water. Thank You for making it possible to study Your Word and feed on it so I can be sustained and strengthened.

When I go to church and ask for Your presence, You bless me. When I rise at morn, labor throughout the day, and lie down at night, You are still with me. I praise You for satisfying my soul. How wonderful it is when I am able to turn to You any time and sense Your holy presence. How great You are for aiding me through the challenges and trials that attack like noontime heat.

Without Your love and friendship, dear Lord, there would be a terrible void in my life nothing else could fill. Your loving-kindness is more wonderful than life itself.

I will bless You, my Lord. I will lift my heart and hands to You from whence comes my help. I will enter Your gates and give thanks to Your name. I will enter Your courts and praise You. You are the living God. You pump life into me each day. Praise be to You, O God!

Thank You, Lord Jesus, as You, the Lamb of God, feed me the water of life. Thank You for satisfying my soul. I praise You for filling me with blessings at Your table, for letting me scoop up living water from Your rivers of delight. Praise You for Your bountiful, measureless blessings.

O God, thou art my God;
early will I seek thee: my soul thirsteth for thee,
my flesh longeth for thee in a dry and thirsty
land, where no water is;
To see thy power and thy glory,
so as I have seen thee in the sanctuary.
Because thy lovingkindness is better than life, my
lips shall praise thee.
Thus will I bless thee while I live:
I will lift up my hands in thy name.
My soul shall be satisfied as with marrow
and fatness; and my mouth shall
praise thee with joyful lips:
When I remember thee upon my bed,
and meditate on thee in the night watches.
Because thou hast been my help,
therefore in the shadow of thy wings
will I rejoice.

PSALM 63:1–7 (KJV)

It Means So Much

A look into my Bible,
    In morning's dewy hour,
For all the day may bring me,
    Will gird my soul with pow'r;
You who have never tried it,
    Know not the help 'twill be;
But, O this word of blessing,
    Means so much to me.

A heart-to-heart communion
    Before the throne of grace,
Reveals to me more clearly
    The sunshine of His face;
You who have never tried it,
    Know not the light 'twill be;
But, O a talk with Jesus,
    Means so much to me.

An all-day walk with Jesus,
    While busy moments fly,
Rejoicing in His service,
    Thro' grace that He'll supply;
You who have never tried it,
    Know not the joy 'twill be;
But, O this life with Jesus,
    Means so much to me.

B. B. Beal, 1916

THE GREATEST FRIEND OF ALL

Most of us are blessed with many friends. However, our close, loyal friends are often only a few. They are like sweet perfume, never fading, near at hand, lingering.

I asked a group of people of all ages to describe their dearest friends. Some of the answers they gave were loving, caring, faithful, honest, empathetic, sharing, listening, trustworthy, cheerful, friends in all kinds of weather.

A few are lifelong friends, our paths crisscrossing and weaving like a tapestry, always caring. Others are separated from us by time and distance. When we get in touch, it's as though we pick up where we left off. There's the cluster of friends who are near us right now, just a phone call or short distance away. All of these friends are to be treasured.

As wonderful as these dear ones are, we have a Friend who surpasses them all. He is our Comforter, the Holy Spirit of God. He cares for us. Not only does He provide for our needs, but He drenches us with unlimited blessings and love. He loves us more than any other possibly can. The Holy Spirit's love goes beyond all limits. It's everlasting, unquenchable. Should we obey and serve God throughout our entire lives, we still haven't earned his love. It's just there. Should we fall into the deepest chasm of trials or depression, others may turn their backs on us in dismay. Still the Holy Spirit is there, loving and helping. Pure. Comforting. Understanding. Enveloping.

This phenomenal person of the triune Godhead stands by us as an ever-faithful friend. When the going gets tough, I visualize myself running and hiding behind His coattail like a child would his big brother.

"You can't get me now!" I find myself shouting at the foes through quivering lips.

He may not always help us solve problems the way we want, but He remains by our side and sees us through.

We might think of our dear friend as One we shouldn't burden too much with our little problems. Unlike some, He never tires of us coming to Him again and again, unloading our worries and cares on His shoulders.

We often hear folks say nothing is too big for God. This is certainly true. I would also add: Nothing is too small for us to bring to Him.

As I drove to work the other day, I spotted a tiny bird fluttering helplessly on the pavement alongside the road. I was running late and unable to stop. I prayed that someone could help it. At the same time a tall, young man was jogging along the sidewalk. I watched in my rearview mirror as he noticed the bird. He stopped, went over, and gently gathered it in his huge hands. *That's the way it is with God,* I thought. Our needs are never too small for Him.

He listens and listens and listens some more. When we cry, I believe He cries with us. When we talk with Him about happy or funny experiences, I believe He laughs. God created us with a terrific sense of humor. Couldn't it be possible that He has one, too? Especially when He made the aardvark!

What I love the most about my friendship with the Holy Spirit is how He knows me through and through. Bob and I have been married almost forty years. We know what the other is going to say or do even before we do it. God knows us more than that. He knows every secret room of our hearts.

When I face the turmoil of decisionmaking and am seeking God's will, I thrash through my doubts, anger, hurts, and despair with Him. He already knows how I feel, so I may as well bring it out so He can help me. Unlike some friends, the problems are never too great that He would turn His back on me.

He is a true and honest friend. I may not like what He is revealing to me, but I know He is right. After I argue, cry, stomp my feet, plead, and pout, I still find

Him there, waiting for me to submit to His right way.

The Holy Spirit is my dearest, closest Friend. I know He is my God and I must honor and worship Him. He surrounds me with love. His strength flows through me. There really is no greater friend than He.

I'm thankful for how He comforts us in grief and sorrow. He intercedes for us to Jesus and God the Father in heaven. He even directs others to be with us in our needs.

What amazes me most is how the Holy Spirit works through people to answer our prayers. Christians are often the tool for God's work. In the same way I prayed for the little bird and someone else came along, He uses us to care, love, and give.

THE BEST FRIEND OF ALL

Do you seek for a friend who is always the
     same,
Who will answer your sigh and your call?
There is just such a Friend, I will tell you His
     name—
It is Jesus, the best Friend of all.

Would you lean on an arm that is able to quell
All the forces of ill that abound?
Grasp the hand that was pierced to remove
     Satan's spell,
And thy soul's dearest refuge is found.

Would you walk day by day in a halo of light,
In the smile of the angels of God?
Would you know the repose that no sorrow can
     blight?
Choose the path your Redeemer has trod.

Would you dwell evermore in the
     mansions above,
Mid the glories that fade not away?
Would you drink endless bliss from the fount
     of His love?
Give your heart to the Savior today.

G. M. BILLS, EARLY 1920S

GENTLE

YOUR GENTLE PRESENCE

Father, thank You for Your gentle presence that ministers to me. I'm grateful for Your comfort, help, and guidance. You show gentleness, even during times of conflict, when I must be firm and stand up for right. I appreciate the way You teach me to do so in a strong but gentle, loving manner.

When I want to strike out at those who are unkind, I praise You for giving me a gentle spirit. Thank You for urging me to pray for wrongdoers to accept You as their Savior. Through this, I am able to be the kind of Christian You want me to be.

Thank You for taking away any resentment I have. I don't understand why good and bad people alike suffer and profit, how You send rain on the just and unjust; but Your compassion for everyone exceeds mine. When I have trouble understanding, I lean on Your wisdom, purpose, and timing. I will not seek revenge or rejoice when those who have done wrong are tangled in their own deceptive webs. Instead, I ask for Your gentle presence once again. Thank You for being a righteous judge.

I'm grateful for You showing me this same gentle way, as I reason with someone. When I have to be firm, I learn to mix in an abundance of love, care, and gentleness.

Thank You, Father, for when You were patient,

gentle, and loving in Bible times to those who stumbled aimlessly. Thank You for showing me this same compassion today. Because of this, You wash away my wrongdoings and give me the new joy of Your Holy Spirit. Your Spirit dwells within, cleanses, and refills me regularly with a fresh, new fullness of life. All of this happens because Your Son, Jesus Christ, gave His all for me. You are so good to each one of us, Father. Your gentleness and care flow through every area of my life. Your mercy endures forever. Because of Your gentle, yet firm love, I want to be a blessing to You in everything I do.

And be kind to one another, tenderhearted, forgiving one another, just as God in Christ forgave you.

 EPHESIANS 4:32 (NKJV)

Firm, Yet Gentle

Seven-year-old Freddie jutted out his lower lip, unwilling to try any longer to solve the new math problems. Once again his teacher, Linda Markwell, firmly yet gently walked him through the steps. After many days of struggling with the new procedure, the two came through with success and a victorious high five.

Freddie was free spirited and stubborn. When pushed the wrong way, he balked. No one became the winner. It took a lot of patience to teach Freddie. He had attention deficit disorder. Instead of breaking his spirit, Linda firmly but gently opened the portals of learning and guided him through.

Freddie appreciated his teacher for that. He learned to follow her lead out of love, respect, and trust.

Years later, a burly, six-foot-five young man came up to Linda in a restaurant and introduced himself.

"Mrs. Markwell? I'm Freddie," he announced with a grin. "You taught me in your class when I was seven years old. Do you remember me?"

Linda had often thought about Freddie through the years. Of course she remembered him and was more than pleased to see him, now a grown man.

Freddie (presently known as Fred) had graduated

from high school, taken extra training, and obtained and held a good job. He told Linda he felt proud of his accomplishments. He also said he never forgot her. She was his favorite teacher.

Linda loves the Lord and prays frequently for her students. Many times God firmly yet gently helps young people through her teaching. Each time Linda thinks of Fred, she has a warm feeling in her heart.

I've often wondered what Fred's life would have been like had it not been for Linda. Perhaps God would have put another "Linda" in his path.

Like Freddie, I, too, am free spirited and can be strong willed. God knows my needs and my weaknesses. He doesn't "bully" or pressure me into making right decisions. Instead, He firmly yet gently nudges my heart as He opens the right portals of my walk with Him and helps me pass through.

We can be thankful for His firm, gentle presence in our lives and those we love and pray for. We can appreciate His directing hand on our Christian teachers, leaders, and parents as they, too, practice His firm and gentle ways.

How Close You Are

How close You are, Lord,
    When evening shadows fall.
Streaks of twilight linger,
    then darkness covers all.

How close You are, Lord!
    I hear Your voice so clear.
I feel Your tender touch,
    Your gentle presence near.

SAVIOR, LIKE A SHEPHERD LEAD US

Savior, like a shepherd lead us,
    Much we need Thy tender care;
In Thy pleasant pastures feed us,
    For our use Thy folds prepare.
Blessed Jesus, blessed Jesus!
    Thou hast bought us, Thine we are.

We are Thine, Thou dost befriend us,
    Be the guardian of our way;
Keep Thy flock, from sin defend us,
    Seek us when we go astray.
Blessed Jesus, blessed Jesus!
    Hear, O hear us when we pray.

DOROTHY ANN THRUPP, 1836

GIVING

The Giver of All

Thank You, Father, for being the giver of all. My possessions, the people I love, the beauties of nature, You are the One who gave them. There would be nothing without You. You made life. You are the beginning. You are the greatest giver.

I praise You for the beauty You furnish us on this earth. The skies, trees, and flowers come from You. The sun, moon, and stars reflect Your handiwork.

Thank You for making me the way I am. You had a plan when You created me. I'm grateful for my family, loved ones, and friends. Thank You for teaching us to love one another. Thank You for Your church, for the strength and encouragement it gives.

I praise You especially for Your pure, everlasting love, for giving Your Son, so I may be a part of the family of God.

Teach me, O Lord, to give with a love like Yours. Guide me, I pray, into ways I can give to others with actions, talents, time, and riches. Let me do these things and give You all the glory.

In Jesus' name, amen.

CRUSHED, BUT STILL GIVING

Ray and Jan loved their work as citywide Christian youth directors. Their group had grown by leaps and bounds. Teenagers one by one accepted Christ. Lives were changed because of Ray and Jan's faithful service in the Lord. Lasting friendships developed.

One afternoon everything took a different turn when a "well-meaning" woman saw Ray in a local restaurant with a woman other than his wife. She witnessed him gazing lovingly at the woman and holding her hands across the table.

Rumors spread like wildfire before Ray and Jan ever knew what was happening. So far no one confronted the couple. Instead, the gossip intensified.

Finally, as news reached the citywide Christian Youth board of directors, the stories had blown way out of proportion. A meeting was called. Ray and Jan were requested to appear before the board.

The board members confronted Ray and Jan with the story. The couple was shocked and hurt.

Ray confirmed the dinner and his love for the woman. After all, she was his sister. She had arrived in town for only a couple of hours. Jan had to work overtime, so Ray had taken his sister out to dinner. His sister was leaving for the mission field, and Ray wouldn't see her again for two years. The board assured them of their support and prayers.

After Ray and Jan went home, Ray changed into old clothes. He decided to take his anger and frustration out on the yard. He jerked and tore at the weeds. He hacked at the dirt, muttering angrily as he worked. Next came the rose bushes. Ray pruned haphazardly at the dead rosebuds, vowing to strike back at the talebearers for hurting him and his wife in such a cruel way. The shears reached too far and lopped off a beautiful multicolored rose. Ray gathered up the flower. Hot tears flowed as he angrily crushed it in a clinched fist. He felt he and his wife had been crushed in the same way.

"How could they, God?" he sobbed aloud. "After all we've done for the kids in this town!"

Cool moisture filled his hand. Ray remembered how Jesus had been mistreated. Jesus never struck back. He just kept loving and giving.

Ray hung his head. As he held the flower, a sweet fragrance from the crushed petals filled his nostrils.

He sensed God urging him not to strike back, but for Jan and him to keep giving and loving. Ray felt a strange peace. God would defend the couple.

Teenagers stepped forward and told Ray's story wherever they went. Ministers called Ray and Jan, saying they would not only pray, but would tell their churches the real story.

Before long, the honorable story spread throughout the city. People from all over asked forgiveness for believing and spreading such rumors. The Christian Youth board rejoiced, glad for believing in the couple's integrity. The woman who started it all tried to explain herself and shifted her interests elsewhere. Ray and Jan forgave her anyway.

Ray and Jan learned a valuable lesson: to trust God at all times, to love and forgive. They decided that in all circumstances, even when crushed, they would follow Christ's example and keep on giving in His service.

But he was pierced for our transgressions,
*   he was crushed for our iniquities;*
the punishment that brought us peace
*   was upon him,*
*   and by his wounds we are healed.*

ISAIAH 53:5 (NIV)

Be imitators of God, therefore, as dearly loved children and live a life of love, just as Christ loved us and gave himself up for us as a fragrant offering and sacrifice to God.

EPHESIANS 5:1–2 (NIV)

GIVE OF YOUR BEST TO THE MASTER

Give of your best to the Master;
    Give of the strength of your youth.
Throw your soul's fresh, glowing ardor
    Into the battle for truth.
Jesus has set the example,
    Dauntless was He, young and brave.
Give Him your loyal devotion;
    Give Him the best that you have.
Give of your best to the Master;
    Give Him first place in your heart.
Give Him first place in your service;
    Consecrate every part.
Give, and to you shall be given;
    God His beloved Son gave.
Gratefully seeking to serve Him,
    Give Him the best that you have.

HOWARD B. GROSE, LATE 1800S

GUIDING

Remarkable Communication

Mark loved his church's adult class. The group often became engaged in lively discussions. Best of all, his teacher challenged the group in their walk with God to make it an everyday experience.

Recently, the class began learning how God could guide them if they would tune in and obey. The teacher passed out devotional books to the group and encouraged them to read a little each day.

"You need to start with prayer, then read your Bible and devotional book every day possible," the teacher announced.

Mark felt this sounded great. He decided to begin immediately. The next morning he awakened a little earlier to take time with God. Mark enjoyed this time, but he felt no special direction from God. The next week Mark told the class what happened. He wanted God to guide him.

Again, the teacher challenged Mark and the class. "The next step is to remember that communication with God needs to go both ways. After you finish praying and reading your Bible, listen with your mind and your heart. You'll be surprised at how God works."

The following morning Mark did exactly as the teacher said. Before long, he felt a guiding presence.

Mark questioned God about different things in his life. He listened for answers. He wanted God to use him more than anything.

When Mark prepared to leave for work one morning, he grabbed his briefcase and newspaper. He always read on the bus. The church devotional book on the coffee table loomed up at him. This time he felt God urging him to take it along.

For the rest of the week, Mark obeyed God's lead. Not only did he read a page from the small book, but he tore the sheet out and left it on the seat before leaving the bus. He continued doing the same thing every day.

"What's so exciting about this?" Mark murmured under his breath.

Tom lived close to town. His fiancée had recently died from a serious heart condition. Tom tried helping with her medical bills. He could barely make ends meet with his current job. Tom was so distraught, he felt like taking his own life. He wondered if there was a God up there who even cared.

Each day Tom boarded the same bus where Mark stepped off. They nodded, barely noticing one another.

One Wednesday Tom boarded the bus. He and Mark happened to sit in the same spot. Tom noticed the paper on the seat. He picked it up and began reading mindlessly. It didn't take long before Tom became interested in the stories.

Weeks went by. Mark faithfully reading the devotions on the way to work and leaving the pages on the seat. Tom continued to find and read them.

Mark continued wondering about God's leading. Was God really guiding him or had it been Mark's imagination all along?

Tom started watching for the papers. His attitude toward life was taking a new turn. He wondered if God really did care about him. Maybe there was something to becoming a Christian.

One day, Mark's work required him to make his first stop at another business farther into town, so he remained on the bus.

Tom climbed on the bus and sat across from Mark. Neither noticed the other. Mark finished the daily reading, tore it out, and placed it on the seat beside him.

"You're the one!" Tom exclaimed. "I've been reading these papers every day. They are giving me hope to go on."

Mark stared with amazement as Tom briefly told him about his fiancée and the hard times. A warm feeling grew inside Mark. He was beginning to understand God's remarkable communication and work.

"Let's get together and talk," Mark urged. "How about one night after work this week?"

Tom agreed wholeheartedly.

Soon after, Tom started going with Mark to the church adult class. Mark also helped Tom find a better job in Mark's company. The two became good friends.

SHIFTING INTO OVERDRIVE

This is one of those hectic days, Lord, when I'm forced to shift into overdrive. I'm meeting myself coming and going. Although the things I must accomplish are good, I'm struggling to keep above all that's happening.

Even though these days are busy, thank You for helping me along the way. I tried to simplify today's schedule ahead of time, but more last-minute little things plopped in my lap. You are so wonderful for granting me a joyful heart and the energy to shift into overdrive so I could make it through successfully.

When I feel like I'm spinning my wheels, You help me along and sometimes give me a little push. When I begin to panic and lose my focus, You remind me of Your calming, guiding presence.

I delight in Your goodness and will strive to walk (or run) in Your footsteps. When I get a little wobbly, I praise You for stabilizing me.

Thank You, Lord, for loving me and helping me relax, for minimizing my frustrations. Each time I listen to Your leading, You seem to add hours to my day.

For this day's help and guidance, I thank You, Lord. Please help tomorrow be a little less hectic so I can shift out of overdrive!

Mountain Trail Guide

The alarm rattled a reminder: Saturday, 5:00 A.M. Paula hit the snooze button with a clumsy hand. Although she was half awake, it didn't take her long to remember the day's upcoming event. She and a group of women would be hiking a six-mile trail near the base of Mount Rainier.

The alarm sounded again. Paula quickly turned it off so her husband could sleep. She slipped into layers of clothing and comfortable hiking shoes, grabbed her backpack and lunch bag, and drove to the church where everyone was to meet.

Soon Paula and her friends climbed into a motor home and drove toward one of Mount Rainier's state parks. By then, everyone was more awake and excited about the hike. They all agreed about how grateful they were to have a woman who knew the area as a guide.

When they pulled into the park, Paula gazed at the huge fir and pine trees surrounding them. She wondered how long it had taken them to grow.

The women started up a winding trail with their guide at the lead. The morning sunlight cast shimmering rays and shadows and sprinkled dewy diamonds on shrubs and flowers. Glistening beaded spider webs with artistic designs decorated the path. The air sang with silence, punctuated by the birds' soft, sweet refrain. The refreshing smell of water, dirt, and plant growth filled Paula's nostrils. She breathed deeply as they walked, savoring each moment.

Farther into the woods they wandered. Once in a while they came upon other hikers who nodded and smiled. By now the sun shone straight above them. It was time to shed jackets and stuff them in their small backpacks.

The trail led toward the edge of a ravine. Paula and her friends took in the view below.

They knew well to walk with caution along the path, now turned rocky. Chipmunks and marmots scampered for safety to nearby crevasses.

The guide found a comfortable spot near some shady trees to take a lunch break. Shy chipmunks finally scurried their way toward the group, awaiting leftover morsels. Pictures were taken to freeze precious memories for a lifetime. Most of the women relaxed. Paula felt restless, filled with excitement and anticipation of what they would find around the next bend.

After lunch, the guide led Paula and the other women higher up the mountain trail. The ravine grew deeper as they walked. The guide reached out to help some women along the precipitous slopes. Before long they learned to help one another.

Soon they came to a long footbridge that crossed the ravine. It swayed slightly, yet it appeared strong enough. Everyone gasped. They all knew they must trust their guide. One by one the women gingerly crossed. Paula started over last.

Paula's hands clasped the bridge's strong cables. The river below roared in her ears. She could see the guide on the other side mouthing for her to keep walking forward. Instead of looking down, Paula kept her gaze on the bridge ahead and the guide coaching her toward the other side. Once across, the river below sounded much friendlier.

They rounded a bend, and the group came to a clearing. There, before them, stood Carbon Glacier in all its wonder. Its massive structure rose before them like an immense dish of vanilla ice cream. It reflected life, danger, and the profound creation of God's handiwork. Paula paused and thanked God.

The trip back seemed quicker. Even the venture over the bridge wasn't as frightening. The sun began sinking behind the trees. Paula pulled out her jacket and slipped it on. She felt chilled. Was it from the cool air or the growing awareness of potential danger of being on the trails after dark? Again, she felt thankful for their guide.

New energy filled the group as they arrived at the park and climbed back in the motor home. They would soon be back to civilization.

Civilization, Paula thought. That's what it's called.

Modern convenience took over as the hungry bunch pulled into a nearby fast-food place, then on to the comforts of home.

The following summer a few of the women decided to follow the same guide on another six-mile hike up Mount Rainier. This time they would start their hike at a lodge and be high enough for snow along the trails. Paula wouldn't miss it for anything.

The sun poured its bright rays on the group. Rocks along the trail reflected the warmth.

Upward Paula and her friends climbed. The valley to the left provided a gorgeous view for miles. Tiny rivers ribboned through the treetops. Steep, rocky banks across the valley accommodated a group of mountain sheep, barely detectable to the human eye. More mountains and hills rose majestically to their right.

Paula appreciated their guide's sure sense of direction. All they had to do was listen and follow her.

When they reached the top of a ridge, the women stared in reverent awe at the magnificent valleys surrounding them. No matter which way they turned, patches of snow, lush grass, rivers, and crevasses stretched for miles. A small outhouse stood precariously on one side of the ridge. Only the bravest would enter.

The group enjoyed lunch and thanked God for the beauty.

Soon this hike also ended. Everyone filtered into the little coffee shop below for hot chocolate and doughnut, then returned home.

You give me your shield of victory,
*   and your right hand sustains me;*
*   you stoop down to make me great.*
You broaden the path beneath me,
*   so that my ankles do not turn.*

Psalm 18:35–36 (niv)

Life's Treks

I often wonder what those hikes would have been like had the women not listened to their guide, or what would have happened if they went with no guide at all. I imagine there could have been a tragedy. Instead, the memories, thrills, and wonders will linger with many for a lifetime.

In our treks through life, we, too, need a guide. This is not a one-day hike. It is life eternal. Our guide must be the all-knowing God.

We learn to listen for His alarm and become aware of His warning and directions. It doesn't take long for us to develop a keen awareness of His guiding presence.

At times we may get caught up in the beauty or the dangers. We hear God's voice reminding us to listen and keep our focus on Him. When we do, He directs us along the right paths and gives us wonderful, lifetime memories.

ONE GOOD THING FOR GOD

Diane could never say no. If her church asked for her to volunteer for something, she was there. When the school PTA asked for help, she committed to one more project. Whenever her husband wanted to invite work associates to dinner, Diane rolled up her sleeves one more notch and pulled out her box of quick, yummy recipes.

Days of shifting herself into overdrive were becoming too commonplace. Diane could see everything she was working on becoming ineffective. She no longer did her best work. Worst of all, Diane had begun feeling as if there was nothing left of herself. She often became irritable and moody. Her energy level dropped drastically. All she wanted to do was sleep. She had burned out.

Diane's husband became concerned. After some coaxing, he convinced her to see a doctor. She reluctantly fit it into her tight schedule. The diagnosis came back. Diane was so run down she was on the edge of completely falling apart physically and emotionally.

Diane's doctor perched on the edge of his desk and gave her a firm look. "How many good books have you wanted to read in the past few years, Diane? I want you to drench yourself in relaxation and moderate exercise. Read your Bible and ask God to help you develop a new lifestyle."

Diane sat before her doctor with slumped shoulders. She knew stress and endless duties needed to be removed from her life.

The next day, with her husband's help, Diane resigned all volunteer positions. Her husband and children helped more around the house. He began taking his important business associates out to dinner.

Diane didn't know how everyone would manage without her. Surprisingly, new people stepped forward. Others had been waiting for a chance to help.

Diane settled in. She rested, read good books, and did some moderate exercise. She prayed and read her Bible. She thought a lot about how God wanted her to plan her activities once she regained her health. God showed Diane how stretching herself too thin was not a part of His will.

Months passed. Diane received the doctor's approval

to take on a little responsibility. Now she knew she couldn't be all things to all people. This time she could choose one good thing for God and do it well.

Now Diane enjoyed her family and life in general more. She also loved having more time for herself and benefiting from God's guidance for a happier, healthier life.

CHANGE

Father, I'm not very good at handling change in my life. Although this transition is for the good, it's still extremely stressful for me. I know I can moan and complain, or I can praise You for it and thank You for the good things to come.

Instead of grumbling and worrying, I wait on You for help and direction. In trials and uncertainties, You defend me. When I need mercy, You meet me with Your love. You know my needs and desires in this change, and I trust You to guide me according to Your will.

You were there in the beginning when the earth's foundation was laid. The heavens were created by Your hands. The trees, birds, and flowers came forth. Now they mature, then grow old and die. Still You are here.

Times change. Circumstances change. When heaven and earth pass away, You shall remain. Through it all, You wrap Your protecting, comforting cloak about me and hold me near. You are the steadfast rock I can cling to. You, Lord, are security. You are the same yesterday, today, and forever.

There was a time You wanted me to change. I balked and stalled, but finally I listened to Your call. Old things in my life passed away, and through You I became brand-new, without sin. I obeyed as You planted Your spiritual seed in the soft soil of my heart, rich and ready to produce for You. Thank You for that change. You created an exciting new life for me.

Now I commit this new change to You, Lord. I know everything works together for good as I continue to love You and obey Your leading.

And we know that in all things God works for the good of those who love him, who have been called according to his purpose.

ROMANS 8:28 (NIV)

A GOOD MIX

Carolyn added a last-minute touch to the floral arrangement she placed before the church pulpit. She checked the communion table with a scrutinizing gaze.

Everything is perfect for tomorrow's worship service, she thought. *Well, almost everything.*

She still wondered why the organ had to be moved. It had been in the same spot for years. The youth group was scheduled to sing in the service. They were so different. They were even bringing in their own instruments. The church congregation was growing fast. Carolyn couldn't sit in her usual pew unless she came early.

She sank to the pew and sighed. "God, what's happening?" she whispered.

As Carolyn prayed, she felt God guide her thoughts to years back when she was a teenager. Gospel quartets had popped up everywhere. She, along with other youth back then, loved the music.

"That was difficult for parents and grandparents to get used to, Lord." She surprised herself by saying her answer out loud.

Before she knew it, Carolyn went to the front of the church and knelt at the well-used altar. She asked God to guide her in having an open, willing heart and to help her accept change. She prayed for God to direct the church leaders in their efforts to hold on to hundreds of years of wonderful church heritage in worship and music. Then she prayed for God to help her to understand and appreciate the needs of the younger people.

Her whispered prayer echoed in the quiet church sanctuary. "I know the youth are our future, Lord. Please guide me in relating to them. Show me how to share the priceless things we've learned through the years; and help me to love, accept, and appreciate these kids."

Carolyn rose from the altar, took a deep breath, and smiled. "I guess I can learn to handle some change, Lord," she said softly. "Help us to work together."

She paused and looked at the organ. "You know, Lord, with a little effort, we all can make a good mix."

At that moment, Carolyn realized that even in change, God is still the same. He loves all kinds of people in all the different stages of life, on into eternity.

O Master,
Let Me Walk with Thee

O Master, let me walk with Thee
    In lowly paths of service free;
Tell me Thy secret; help me bear
    The strain of toil, the fret of care.

HENRY PERCY SMITH, 1874

HEALING

Your Healing Presence

I bring this condition of mine to You, Lord Jesus. I ask for Your healing presence. I don't know how You will work in my life, but I trust You unconditionally.

Once You prayed in the Garden of Gethsemane for Your Father to take the cup of suffering and death from You. Still, You placed Your love and trust in Him. You asked not for Your will to be done, but Your Father's, instead.

I don't know how or when You will touch me. I only know You are with me, Lord. You supply my needs. You give me peace. You are my peace.

My strength ebbs to near nothing. I feel I can't hold on much longer, but You remind me how in these times You are strong for me.

Let me pour out my troubles to You each day, dear Lord. Others may sometimes tire of hearing my complaints. You, my Lord, always listen, understand, and care. You give me strength for each day.

I know Your healing presence is with me right now. I yield to You, Lord, and give You control of my entire being. Continue to surround me and fill me with Your Holy Spirit. Take this cup from me. Heal me, I pray. In all things, may Your will be done.

I know You love me. I also realize without a doubt

that You take my needs and concerns to heart, and You want what is best for me.

Thank You, Lord Jesus, for Your healing presence. Because of Your love, let me be a living demonstration of Your power and give You all the praise.

> *Surely he took up our infirmities*
> *and carried our sorrows,*
> *yet we considered him stricken by God,*
> *smitten by him, and afflicted.*
> *But he was pierced for our trangressions,*
> *he was crushed for our iniquities;*
> *the punishment that brought us peace*
> *was upon him,*
> *and by his wounds we are healed.*
> *We all, like sheep, have gone astray,*
> *each of us has turned to his own way;*
> *and the LORD has laid on him*
> *the iniquity of us all.*

ISAIAH 53:4–6 (NIV)

Healing of the Heart

Misty's stormy years as a teenager had taken their toll. Now twenty-three, she still couldn't get over the stigma of being the "black sheep" in the family. Harsh words and unkind actions by both daughter and parents left scars, threatening never to heal.

Misty had become a Christian and changed her life, but the black sheep stigma still remained. Each time she saw her parents or talked with them by phone, her hurts returned. Although her mother and father said they loved her and were proud of her, the anger and injured feelings wouldn't leave.

My parents tell me they love me, she pondered. *They say they forgive me for the past. They even ask me to forgive them.* Misty couldn't understand why the pain would not leave.

Finally, she took it to the Lord in serious prayer. She looked up scriptures on God healing those in pain. Misty began praying that God would heal her wounds. She asked Him to help her forgive her parents for their unkind words and deeds. Whenever the pain tried to return, she went to the Lord and left it with Him.

How could she make everything up to them? Misty would buy them everything in the world if that would help. God spoke to her again. He touched Misty's wounded soul. He reminded her that her mother and father had already forgiven her. Now God asked Misty to take the final step. She must forgive herself.

Tears flowed. Cleansing confession poured out from Misty to her Savior. She finally turned to her inner self and forgave. The transformation and healing were complete. Misty felt the peace she had longed to feel for so long.

From then on, phone calls with Mom and Dad warmed her heart. She really wasn't the black sheep. Instead, she had been the little wounded lamb. Now Jesus, the real Lamb of God, healed and made her happy and whole.

The next day John saw Jesus coming toward him, and said, "Behold! The Lamb of God who takes away the sin [and pain] of the world!"

JOHN 1:29 (NKJV)

Expecting a Miracle

Have you ever prayed for yourself or someone else to be healed and never expected it to happen? Some may have while praying for Ann.

Ann was pregnant with her third baby. She felt more tired than usual but thought her weariness came from being a busy mother of two growing youngsters. Ann's husband, Bill, worked long hours as a truck driver, so the young mother carried out most household and child-rearing duties.

Ann began feeling intense heartburn and loss of appetite. Her weight suddenly dropped ten pounds, yet she still didn't suspect a problem. The fatigue grew worse. A friend noticed Ann's skin was becoming jaundiced. A trip to the doctor revealed a serious problem. Ann was suffering from severe hepatitis A and B. Being pregnant weakened her body to where she couldn't even lift ten pounds.

Doctors hospitalized Ann immediately. Her husband, children, and friends feared for her life. Ann's family desperately wanted her home and well.

Ann and the doctors were perplexed as to where she had been infected with the terrible disease. The answer never came.

Relatives and friends were alerted to stand by and

pray. Ann feared for the well-being of her unborn child and often lay quietly to feel him move. She sensed God's closeness more than ever before in her life.

Days in the hospital bustled with doctors and nurses. Technicians frequently drew blood. Nights were long. Ann often felt as if her blood was racing through her veins. A few times she almost drifted into unconsciousness, but God's healing presence filled the room and enveloped her in His love. Ann felt it would have been so easy to slip off and go home with the Lord. Each time she began to fade, God brought Bill and her children to mind and Ann struggled for survival.

The saints continued praying, some expecting a miracle. Strangely enough, one small prayer group considered Ann's condition hopeless. They gave up praying for her, saying she would probably die anyway.

Ann's condition worsened. Her skin turned a bright yellow. She communed with God on a closer level than ever. God showed Ann His plan for her to serve Him. He wanted her to live many more years.

Finally, she made a turn for the better. The doctors informed Ann and Bill that she could return home to her family, but she would carry hepatitis in her bloodstream for the rest of her life. From then on, Ann would have to take good care of herself.

A few months later she gave birth to a healthy, adorable baby boy. He was born one month early. After that, Ann regained her strength quickly. People referred to them as the miracle mother and baby. The doubting prayer group learned a surprising lesson on faith, miracles, and healing.

Several years later, Ann went into teaching. Twenty years into her teaching career, news came that all educators were being strongly advised to be vaccinated for hepatitis B for their own protection.

Ann informed the school nurse that this was not necessary for her. When she told the nurse she once had hepatitis A and B while being pregnant, the nurse wouldn't believe her and said Ann couldn't have survived something that serious.

To be certain, Ann went to her local doctor for a blood test. It showed her bloodstream was still filled with hepatitis B, even though she was now healthy and strong.

How was this possible? The saints prayed and believed. Ann trusted God and nestled in His healing, loving presence. God had a calling for Ann to touch the lives of countless children.

Ann is still well, teaching and serving God!

In all things, in God's plan, nothing is impossible when we put our trust in Him!

Just then a woman who had been subject to bleeding for twelve years came up behind him and touched the edge of his cloak. She said to herself, "If I only touch his cloak, I will be healed."

MATTHEW 9:20–21 (NIV)

"Who touched me?" Jesus asked. . . . "Someone touched me; I know that power has gone out from me."

Then the woman, seeing that she could not go unnoticed, came trembling and fell at his feet. In the presence of all the people, she told why she had touched him and how she had been instantly healed. Then he said to her, "Daughter, your faith has healed you. Go in peace."

LUKE 8:45–48 (NIV)

Jesus, Thy Boundless Love to Me

Jesus, Thy boundless love to me
    No thought can reach, no tongue declare;
Unite my thankful heart with Thee
    And reign without a rival there.
To Thee alone, dear Lord, I live;
    Myself to Thee, dear Lord, I give.
O love, how cheering is thy ray!
    All pain before thy presence flies;
Care, anguish, sorrow, melt away
    Wherever thy healing beams arise.
O Jesus, nothing may I see,
    Nothing desire or seek, but Thee!

Paul Gerhardt, 1653
Translated by John Wesley, 1739

HEAVENLY

GOD'S HEAVENLY PRESENCE

What will it be like when our time on this earth is finished and God is ready to take us home?

One of Peter Marshall's sermons to a group of cadets describes it simply. We are reminded of when, as small children, we fell asleep somewhere other than our own beds. Mother or Father gathered us up in strong arms, dressed us in our nightclothes, and gently tucked us into our beds.

Dr. Marshall went on to explain that when we as Christians die, we waken in another room that Jesus has lovingly prepared for us.

WHAT IS HEAVEN LIKE?

What is heaven like? I believe it will be filled with God's enveloping, awesome, unconditional love. A love so perfect no one will hesitate to pass it on to every single soul. There will be no hurt feelings, no skepticism. Each one will love and truly care about everyone else and be showered by God's love.

In this frightening world of violence and disaster, where the poor and uneducated suffer endlessly, our society finds it increasingly difficult to understand and love them. Some we even fear. We keep trying desperately to find the answers, but often come out frustrated.

Sharp, talented, charming, beautiful, and good people are more easily accepted and loved. This is how our world often views things.

God sees it all differently. He cares for the bright, wealthy, and beautiful; He also loves the poor, underprivileged, unattractive, ill-clad, and homeless with an equal, pure love. All of God's children in heaven will be able to love in this way. No more deception. No classes— rich or poor. We'll all be His children. Strong, healthy, worshiping God and basking in His awesome presence.

Oh, the joy we'll share as we unite with each other and see our God and His Son face-to-face!

The Sweetest Music

The sweetest music is not the peal of marriage bells, nor tender descants in moonlight woods, nor trumpet notes of victory—it is the soul's welcome to heaven. God grant that when we die there may not come booming to our ear the dreadful sound, "Depart!" But may we hear stealing upon the air the mellow chime of all the celestial bells saying, "Come, come, come, ye blessed, enter ye into the joy of your Lord!"

Henry Ward Beecher

SHALL WE GATHER AT THE RIVER?

Shall we gather at the river,
    Where bright angel feet have trod,
With its crystal tide forever
    Flowing by the throne of God?

On the margin of the river,
    Washing up its silver spray,
We will walk and worship ever,
    All the happy, golden day.

Ere we reach the shining river,
    Lay we every burden down;
Grace our spirits will deliver,
    And provide a robe and crown.

At the smiling of the river,
    Mirror of the Savior's face,
Saints, whom death will never sever,
    Lift their songs of saving grace.

ROBERT LOWRY, 1864

I did not see a temple in the city, because the Lord God Almighty and the Lamb are its temple. The city does not need the sun or the moon to shine on it, for the glory of God gives it light, and the Lamb is its lamp. The nations will walk by its light, and the kings of the earth will bring their splendor into it. On no day will its gates ever be shut, for there will be no night there. The glory and honor of the nations will be brought into it. Nothing impure will ever enter it, nor will anyone who does what is shameful or deceitful, but only those whose names are written in the Lamb's book of life.

REVELATION 21:22–27 (NIV)

PROTECTING

PROTECTION FROM DANGER

This situation terrified me, Father. I know You must have been with me. Can anything snatch me from You? No. I thank You for surrounding me within Your protecting arms when I was in danger. You made me alert and gave me wisdom and caution.

I praise You for how Your angels encamped about me once again and delivered me from harm. I wonder what Your angels look like. Do they dress a certain way? Do they draw shining swords and surround me? Or do they look like ordinary people?

Because You are my Lord, I shall not fear. You are near, guarding and guiding me all the way. Thank You for never sleeping or turning Your back on me. I will tell everyone I know You are my Savior, my Protector, my Mighty God.

After this moment of danger, I sigh with relief and praise You for taking my hand and leading me to safety.

HIS RESCUING HAND

Several years ago, my son, Dave, our church youth group, and I took a mission trip to San Quintine, Mexico. The entire stay was filled with rewards as we assisted with construction, plumbing, and odd jobs. During the afternoons and evenings we ministered to children and adults in nearby villages.

On the way home, we had a chance to swim in the Gulf of Mexico. One of the teenage girls gave me a crash course in bodysurfing. Each time a huge wave came in, we flopped on our bellies and floated out with the tide. When we could float no farther, we ran back to shore and did it again.

The teenager rode the waves with ease. Every time I tried, I managed to swallow water and came up sputtering. The first thing I would see was the girl's hand reaching out to me, helping me up so I could try it again.

That's the way it is in our lives. When the seas of life get wild, we think we can ride them out with all our skills. Instead, we often come up coughing and sputtering. We find Jesus' hand reaching out over and over to help us.

Thank You, Jesus, for Your helping hand.

The Tallest Lady Ever Seen

Our six-year-old son, Jonny, had been waiting impatiently for his first bike. Living on a busy street corner delayed his getting one. Plans were already in the works for our family to move to a quieter city and street where it would be safer for him to ride.

We didn't know at the time that Jonny was having repeated dreams about a bike accident. He dreamed he was riding with a friend, whom he had never seen before. It always ended with him flying over the handlebars.

After our move, Jonny got his bike. He was a little shaky but did fairly well on quiet streets. One day he and his new friend, Mike, rode their bikes halfway around the block to a cul-de-sac. At the time, I was in the kitchen cooking dinner. All of a sudden, I heard Jonny's screams as he approached our front door.

The door flew open, and I heard a woman calmly tell him, "It's all right. You're home now. You're going to be all right."

I rushed to the living room. Jonny was extremely frightened, his face covered with blood. I eased him to the couch and hurried to the door to thank the woman for bringing him home. I glanced up and down the street, but I couldn't see her anywhere.

Jonny sobbed uncontrollably. He shook so hard he couldn't talk. Bob and I hurried him to the hospital emergency room. The nurse wheeled him off immediately off for X-rays while we waited anxiously for Jonny's return.

After he was wheeled back, we gazed at our little boy. Once filled with fun and enthusiasm, Jonny looked tiny and helpless under the cool sheet. Bob and I took his hands and prayed for him to be well and calm. Jonny finally started to relax. He explained that while he and Mike were riding, their bicycle wheels tangled. Jonny lost his balance and flew over the handlebars.

Jonny paused, and a peaceful look came over him. "Mom and Dad, the tallest lady I ever saw came over to me. She was nice and was very strong when she helped me up. She kept talking with me while she walked me home. Mike was so scared that he followed from behind. Then he ran home to his house."

Jonny told us about his dreams. He realized now that Mike had been the boy he had dreamed about.

We were thankful when we found out Jonny had only a broken nose and no other serious injuries.

Weeks passed and Jonny mended nicely. All he could talk about was the nice, tall lady. If she hadn't been there, we wondered if Jonny might have gone into shock.

Jonny rode his bike to the area of the accident in search of the woman to thank her. He knocked on doors and asked neighbors, but couldn't find the woman.

Mike and Jonny never talked about the accident. Mike moved to a different area, and the boys didn't see each other for several years. One day their paths crossed. In their conversation, Jonny (now Jon) mentioned the bike accident and the tall woman he could never thank.

Mike looked awestruck. "I thought you were talking to yourself. Jon, there was no lady walking you home!"

The boys stood and stared at each other in amazement. Jonny knew the tall woman had helped him, and I heard her talking at our front door.

We don't know the answers, that but we do know that God watched over our six-year-old son that day.

The angel of the LORD encamps around those who fear him, and he delivers them.

PSALM 34:7 (NIV)

IN THE NAME OF JESUS

Warm evening air blew softly through Hannah and George's open bedroom window, lazily stirring the curtains.

The elderly couple had lived in their home a lifetime. The neighborhood always remained close, people watching out for one another. This night seemed no different. The lifelong couple settled into bed to read, ready for a restful night.

A stir outside their window invaded their silence. Hannah glanced up from her book.

"Probably a cat," George assured her. "I'll check anyway."

Before George could reach the window, a young man clambered through and bolted toward him. The speed of the man's body was so intense that when he hit George, both men crashed against the bed. Hannah screamed in terror. Although a stocking cap covered the man's head and face, it was easy to see anger in his eyes, his mouth rigidly set in a thin, tight line.

The man raised his hand to deliver a crushing blow to George's head. "Give me your money and jewelry or I'll beat you and your wife to death!" he growled.

George struggled to no avail.

Hannah bolted upright in bed. "Jesus, help us!"

she shouted with authority. "In Jesus' name, we ask for Your help!"

The man backed toward the window with fright. He stretched his arms out in front of him with his palms facing the couple. "Don't say that," he panted. "I—I won't touch you."

The man stumbled out the window. The couple could hear footsteps running and immediately called the police.

From then on, the couple locked their windows. Hannah and George still thank God for His protection and care that night.

IN THE HOLLOW OF HIS HAND

In the hollow of His hand He will hide me
    When doubt and sin draw near,
Tho' no earthly friend may walk beside me
    I rest secure from fear.

In the hollow of His hand He will hide me
    When the storms of life sweep by,
To the harbor safe He will guide me
    Where His blessed islands lie.

I know whate'er betide me
    His hand will safely guide me,
His love will ever hide me
    In the hollow of His hand.

FLORENCE JONES KADLEY,
CARROLL KING,
SAMUEL W. BEAZLEY, 1914

RESTORING

FROM ASHES TO BEAUTY

Steve and Susan tucked their two young children into bed in their Seattle area home. It was two days after Christmas. Steve's mother and father had come for a visit. The next day Steve's brother would arrive by plane. Steve's parents settled into a guest bed around the corner from the den and fireplace.

The following morning the family had a late breakfast. They planned to pick Steve's brother up from the airport, drive to Olympia, and join other family members. Susan asked a neighbor to watch their home. She left emergency phone numbers, and they were off.

The trip to Olympia didn't take long. When the family walked in the front door, the phone was ringing. It was for Steve. He answered and looked shocked as he listened.

Within an hour after Steve and Susan had left home, the house burst into flames.

Several neighbors saw one hundred-foot flames and billowing smoke. They immediately called 911. Everyone pitched in by doing whatever they could to help.

Firemen arrived within five minutes. The fire crew made quick, wise choices. They managed to put the fire out in about ten minutes before two more units arrived.

When the firemen were able to enter and check for people, they discovered the smoke alarm had malfunctioned. If the blaze had started at night, there would have been no warning. The fire apparently came from the fireplace.

When the fire investigators removed the bricks from the fireplace box, it revealed a wooden frame that had heated and cooled repeatedly over a period of weeks or possibly months. Investigators believed this ultimately led to the wall smoldering. No one knew it was happening or that it could just burst into open flames.

When Steve and Susan purchased their home, the zero clearance fireplace had passed the safety inspection. Because of this, the couple felt safe.

Steve and Susan returned home immediately. They were greeted in their yard by investigating firemen, neighbors, and friends.

They stood back on the corner and looked at what remained. They were thankful for the lives of their family. God was showing them what is really important. Many provided the family with gifts, food, lodging, child care, and overwhelming love. Two days later the couple were able to enter the house with the smokebuster crew. They walked from room to room and identified the items they cherished and the family wanted to restore.

Susan felt mostly concerned about family pictures they had placed in the pantry. The hollow core door had buffeted the fire. The outside was burned off, the top and varnish on the inside of the door, bubbled. Susan had put the pictures in a plastic bin. The pictures received some smoke damage but were restorable.

Steve and Susan walked into the family room where the fireplace had been. About three or four feet away from the fireplace stood a family entertainment center about six feet high. The top half had held a TV, now gone. The bottom half had four shelves. The top shelf held five homemade videos of the children's earlier years. They had been covered by paper. The family movies were a little battered, but later successfully transferred to VHS. The shelves below held a variety of commercial video movies that were melted.

Their walk continued to the dining room. A built-in sideboard buffet stood along one wall, now in charred, black pieces. One drawer held the beginning stages of blueprints—the couple had been remodeling their house. Susan had to pry the drawer open with a fork. The blueprints were singed but legible.

Steve and Susan had kept a photo log of all their remodeling completed in the next drawer down. The pictures and the log were restorable.

A "Hallelujah" calligraphy print by Timothy Bach had been hanging above the fireplace. Three weeks before, Steve and Susan had decided to move the print to the den. The metal frame was melted by heat, had fallen, and lay in broken black glass; but the print itself could be restored.

Before the fire, Steve and Susan's basement had been used for a Young Life group for forty to ninety kids. The fire happened during the kids' Christmas break. By the time the group was due to return, the basement was ready to use.

The incredible part of Steve and Susan's experience was how they recently had taught a six-week course at their church about *affluenza*, a word characterizing our society's need to acquire more and more material things.

Steve and Susan like nice things. They feel the lesson about affluenza came through loud and clear and helped prepare and give them perspective of what was really most important.

Before the fire, Susan's college-age discipleship group had decided to watch one of the videos about affluenza and discuss God's priorities of material belongings. Susan had stored the tape in the buffet.

Another teacher at church wanted to borrow the tape. By then the buffet pieces lay strewn in their yard.

Through everything that had happened, Steve and Susan's faith had grown stronger. They knew, somehow, God had saved the tape. Sure enough, one buffet piece in the yard contained the tape on affluenza. They opened the battered container. The tape, wet from fire hoses, lay inside. The couple dried it out, placed it in a VCR, and it came out clear!

Now Steve and Susan's home is in the process of being rebuilt. Through all this, they have been able to tell others about God's miraculous, restoring touch. Many lives are being blessed and changed because of Steve and Susan's story. The couple is thankful that God spared their family, brought beauty from devastating ashes, and showed them what is most important: His love and the love they have for one another.

Used by permission from
SUSAN ALLSOP

THE MASTER'S TOUCH

Do you remember the poem "The Touch of the Master's Hand" by Myra Brooks Welch? It tells about an auction where an old violin was up for bids. The auctioneer called for offers. It didn't appear to be worth much. The bids slowly came in: one dollar, two dollars, three dollars.

Then an older gentleman came forward. His expert fingers picked up the old instrument. He carefully tuned it. A questioning hush fell in the auction house. The man probably closed his eyes to feel the music. He began to play. The melody came forth sweet and pure, as though sent straight from heaven.

Without a word, the man handed the violin back to the auctioneer. Electricity filled the air. Bids rattled in like firecrackers: hundreds, thousands!

"Sold to the highest bidder!"

What changed it all? The master's touch. The violin appeared worthless. The master musician made the difference.

You may be beaten and worn like that old violin. Perhaps your self-worth has been crushed to where almost nothing is left. God still sees priceless value in you. Let Him touch and restore your body, mind, and soul so that He may use you to glorify Him and give you a joy-filled life.

God can take our broken lives and bring forth the true priceless value He sees in us.

Thank Him for His restoring presence. Give Him praise and glory with all your might as long as you live. In spite of physical afflictions, pain, circumstances, or even growing older, we must further God's kingdom and rely on His restoring touch.

ANOTHER MASTER'S TOUCH

Many years ago Gibson Company not only made Gibson guitars, but another brand called Kalamazoo. My father-in-law bought one of these guitars in approximately 1937, when he was about twenty years old. He carefully kept it in a corner for years. It was seldom played. It didn't seem to be worth much, but the sentimental value made the guitar priceless to my husband, Bob.

Bob loves to play the guitar. For a long time he hoped Dad would pass the guitar on to him. Finally, Dad did. Bob was delighted.

The neck was bent. The strings weren't very good. Bob could barely play it. Yet he saw past all that and visualized more for the old guitar.

Jim, a longtime friend, came to visit us from southern Oregon. He loved fiddles, guitars, bluegrass, and old country music. Jim gathered up the guitar and took it back to his home. He found a master at repairing guitars and placed the Kalamazoo in the repairman's hands.

A month went by. Two months. Three. Jim returned for another visit. He handed Bob the guitar. It sounded like new. Bob certainly was grateful to Jim and his guitar-restoring friend.

It seemed like forever, waiting to have that Kalamazoo fixed. It took time, just as in our lives it takes time to fix things.

God surrounds us with His restoring presence. He has a purpose. He has His own perfect timing in the circumstances of our lives. We need to be patient with others, ourselves, and especially with our all-knowing God. Life is a process. God is in no way finished with us yet.

Let's keep praising Him for His presence, His touch, and His timing. He loves us and knows what is best.

SURPRISING

YOUR SURPRISING PRESENCE

I was so busy today, Lord, going full-speed ahead, keeping all my goals in a nice, neat row. Then it happened. Circumstances changed everything.

Thank You, once again, for helping me remember You are really in charge. Thank You for interrupting my busy thoughts and letting me know Your plan.

I never cease to be amazed at the perfect, yet unexplainable, ways You work. How did this happen, Lord? I can't understand it. Thank You for Your surprising presence and Your marvelous ways.

> *Great is the LORD and most worthy of praise; his greatness no one can fathom.*
>
> PSALM 145:3 (NIV)

BUNS AND HOT DOGS

Tammy and the school PTA fund-raising committee were well organized for the fast-approaching barbecue. They had purchased 250 hot dogs and 250 hot dog buns, hoping to have a successful annual event.

At the same time, the local food bank's supply had become desperately low. Their freezer was empty. Food bank employees and volunteers hoped and prayed for help in meeting the needs of many hungry people.

The day of the PTA barbecue arrived. Volunteers optimistically heated grills, set up condiments, and had the hot dogs and buns ready in the school refrigerator. People came and ate two hundred hot dogs.

At the end of the day, Tammy and the committee did a final inventory of the unsold hot dogs and buns in the school refrigerator. Fifty buns. Correct. Two hundred hot dogs! How can this be? They had begun with 250 and sold 200!

Tammy contacted the school's head cook to see if they also had some hot dogs in the refrigerator. The answer was no. The astonished committee had no idea where the additional 150 hot dogs came from.

After some discussion, Tammy and the others decided to take the leftover food to the local food bank. (They had no idea that the food bank was in serious need.) The PTA volunteers loaded buns and hot dogs into a car and headed out. Minutes before their arrival, a truck from a local bakery dropped off 150 hot dog buns at the same food bank. When Tammy and the crew arrived with 200 hot dogs and 50 buns, they were greeted with big smiles. The food bank volunteers were thrilled and grateful they had something to offer needy families.

Wonderful parents and teachers work in this public school. A lot of them are Christians, including Tammy. Tammy felt that God had planned for them to donate the leftovers to the food bank all along. Many wonder if God multiplied hot dogs and even sent the bread truck to help feed 150 hungry people the same way He had blessed and multiplied loaves and fishes to feed the five thousand.

Used by permission from
TAMMY WHITE

SURPRISING STRING OF FISH

Jack, his wife, Barb, and another couple took a break from college studies and decided to go fishing. A friend loaned them a boat to take to a nearby lake.

Although the outing sounded like fun, it was an important event. The two couples were fishing for more than sport. They needed fish for meals.

Several hours passed. They wondered how all those fish could simply disappear. The four took turns rowing quietly to likely spots. Still, no fish.

Time came to return to shore. They were all disappointed. Jack rowed with slumped shoulders.

"We came to catch fish," Barb announced with determination. "I'm going to pray for God to meet our needs!"

Jack gave Barb a quizzical look. "Come on, Barb. We've put our poles away and are heading in. How can we get fish?"

Barb shook her head and answered, more determined than ever. "I just know God will provide." She bowed her head and prayed silently.

All three people joined her in prayer but wondered how God could answer such a request. They humored Barb, yet a feeling of expectancy filled the air.

They drew closer to shore and pulled the boat in.

A woman and boy stood on the bank as though they had been waiting for the two couples' arrival. The boy held a long string of fish.

The woman walked to Barb and smiled. "Would you folks like some fish? My son and I enjoy fishing, but we don't like eating our catch."

Barb expressed her thanks. The others looked dumbfounded and nodded a hearty appreciation.

On the way home, Jack, Barb, and their friends thanked God for the surprising string of fish and for the wonderful ways He works.

A Different Kind of Fish

Jesus talked with men who made their living by fishing. They became His followers and learned how to become fishers of men.

Jesus must have surprised the disciples when He helped them catch so many fish that their boats almost sank. He probably astounded them more when He helped them fish for men and women to be followers of Christ.

How awesome it is when we pray for God to help us fish for people to accept Him. He quickens our senses so we become keenly aware of others' needs. Then the time comes when we get to draw one after another into God's loving presence and lead them to Him.

When this happens, we never cease to be amazed at how God works. Seeing a soul coming to Christ is as great a thrill as witnessing the birth of a newborn baby.

The next time you ask God to help you win someone to Christ, watch for the surprising way He works. Then be ready and willing to reel that person in for Him!

TRUST AND OBEY

When we walk with the Lord
In the light of His Word,
What a glory He sheds on our way!
While we do His good will, He abides with us
    still,
And with all who will trust and obey.

Trust and obey, for there's no other way
To be happy in Jesus, but to trust and obey.

JOHN H. SAMMIS, 1887

UNDERSTANDING

DO YOU REALLY UNDERSTAND?

Father, there are times I don't know if anyone understands how I feel. I'm frustrated, and I don't know which way to turn. I feel so alone.

My Bible tells me You understand every part of my life. Do You really understand, Father? Do You know what it's like to bring a newborn into this world and fall hopelessly in love with that tiny face? Do you understand how I feel being up all night with a sick child or pacing the floor at 2:00 A.M., when my teenager's out past curfew? Do You see my heart sink when my child presses toward adulthood and leaves the nest?

As I pour my heart out to You, Your warm, soothing presence surrounds me. Your understanding way gives peace to my troubled soul.

Thank You, Father, for caring. Thank You for helping me see how Your Son intercedes for my needs and prayers and helps bring new souls born into Your kingdom.

I can imagine even the angels standing and singing in celebration about Your love and understanding ways. Your love must go way beyond what I am capable of.

Thank You for how Jesus rose in the early morning hours and prayed for each one of us throughout eternity.

I praise You for how He stayed awake in the Garden of Gethsemane and prayed for us, when He faced far more than I can ever imagine.

Thank You, Father, for the understanding Jesus showed when He told the story of the prodigal son, about love and forgiveness.

You really do understand how I feel, don't You, Father? Though my trials and triumphs aren't nearly as great as those of my Savior, I thank You for being here now and understanding me.

O LORD, thou hast searched me, and
*   known me.*
Thou knowest my downsitting and mine uprising,
*   thou understandest my thought afar off.*
Thou compassest my path and my lying down,
*   and art acquainted with all my ways.*
For there is not a word in my tongue,
*   but, lo, O LORD, thou knowest it*
*   altogether.*
Thou hast beset me behind and before,
*   and laid thine hand upon me.*
Such knowledge is too wonderful for me;
*   it is high, I cannot attain unto it.*

PSALM 139:1–6 (KJV)

UNDERSTANDING THE CRAVINGS

Many students who put themselves through college don't have it easy. Jack and Barb certainly fit into that category.

Along with studying for the ministry, the young couple learned how to trust God for their daily needs. Their prayer life grew stronger as God understood and helped them.

At the time, Jack and Barb were expecting their first child. Being a student minister's wife on a limited budget didn't exclude Barb from having the pregnant mother cravings. She wanted an apple so badly, she could taste it.

As always, she took her need to the Lord in prayer and asked for one red delicious apple. After some thought, Barb decided to go back to prayer and apologize for being so picky. She asked God, instead, to give her any kind of apple He wanted her to have. Then she thanked God, trusted Him for the answer to come, and began cleaning house.

Before long, Barb heard a knock at their small college apartment door. When she answered it, Barb was greeted by a kind man the couple knew. He had two big boxes sitting in front of her doorway filled to the tops with red and yellow delicious apples!

Needless to say, Barb thanked God for not only providing for her needs but understanding how she felt.

S-T-O-P

At times we feel we have a corner on all our off days, mixed emotions, and concerns in our lives. The wonderful part is how much God understands how we feel. After all, He made us.

He knows us through and through. He cares about every area of our lives and is willing to help and guide when we ask.

Our lives aren't too minute for Him to care, because He loves us more than anyone in this world can possibly love. He's all-knowing, just, and understanding. He sees what is best for us even when we don't recognize the answers ourselves.

The next time an off day hits, remember to S-T-O-P:

Stop and pray.

Tell Him how you feel, then listen to Him.

Open your heart to His presence.

Praise Him for His help and understanding.

*Do not be anxious about anything, but in
everything, by prayer and petition, with
thanksgiving, present your requests to God.
And the peace of God, which transcends all
understanding, will guard your hearts and your
minds in Christ Jesus.*

*Finally, brothers [and sisters], whatever is true,
whatever is noble, whatever is right, whatever is
pure, whatever is lovely, whatever is admirable—if
anything is excellent or praiseworthy—think about
such things. Whatever you have learned or received
or heard from me, or seen in me—put it into
practice. And the God of peace will be with you.*

PHILIPPIANS 4:6–9 (NIV)

ALSO FROM
ANITA CORRINE DONIHUE

WHEN I'M ON
MY KNEES

ISBN: 978-1-59789-694-8
256 pages, $5.97

WHEN I'M
PRAISING GOD

ISBN: 978-1-59789-702-0
256 pages, $5.97

LORD, I NEED
YOUR BLESSING

ISBN: 978-1-59789-246-9
256 pages, $5.97

Available wherever books are sold.